THE WOMAN WHO SPLIT THE ATOM

LISE MEITNER

BY MARISSA MOSS

ABRAMS BOOKS FOR YOUNG READERS
NEW YORK

The illustrations in this book were made with pen, ink, and watercolor wash.

See page 251 for photography credits.

Cataloging-in-Publication Data has been applied for and
may be obtained from the Library of Congress.

ISBN 978-1-4197-5853-9

Edited by Howard W. Reeves
Book design by Heather Kelly

Published in 2022 by Abrams Books for Young Readers, an imprint of ABRAMS.

Printed and bound in U.S.A.
10 9 8 7 6 5 4 3 2 1

Abrams Books for Young Readers are available at special discounts when purchased in quantity for premiums and promotions as well as fundraising or educational use. Special editions can also be created to specification. For details, contact specialsales@abramsbooks.com or the address below.

ABRAMS The Art of Books
195 Broadway, New York, NY 10007
abramsbooks.com

TO WARREN HECKROTTE,

with deep gratitude for his help in understanding nuclear physics. Warren was a nuclear physicist who worked at Lawrence Livermore National Laboratory and was involved in nuclear weapons talks with the Soviets under five different presidents, starting with John F. Kennedy, ending with Bill Clinton. Warren knew personally many of the physicists mentioned in this book and gave me access to his personal library of books and documents about the history of nuclear fission. Sadly, Warren died before the manuscript was finished, but we spent many hours together at his dining room table, hashing through different aspects of Meitner's story and the science and personalities behind it.

CONTENTS

ONE

DREAMS OF THE IMPOSSIBLE

BERLIN, 1938
What if they ask for my passport, the one I don't have? Can they tell I'm Jewish? Do I look like I'm escaping?
Oh, why did I wait so long to leave?
Should I have tried to disguise myself?
Too late now . . .
Papers!
Papers!

Lise Meitner was an internationally recognized scientist. She'd fought hard as a girl to get an education and as a young woman to find a position. It had been a long struggle to be taken seriously as a physicist.

How could I leave the institute when finally, FINALLY, it didn't matter that I'm a woman?
Now all that matters is that I'm a Jew.

As a girl, being a scientist had seemed impossible . . .

Lise Meitner had thought of herself as a completely ordinary little girl, a girl who happened to sleep with a math book under her pillow, as if the equations would slip into her head overnight. Instead of reading novels or poetry like her sisters, she read about the quadratic formula, about figuring out the volume of a cone, about plotting a parabola on a grid. Her brain was full of questions, and she had to know the answers.

Her parents encouraged her curiosity. They wanted all eight of their children to think about the world and follow their interests. For them, the late 1800s were exciting years to be in Vienna. Meitner's mother had come from Russia, her father from Czechoslovakia. Both were places where Jews couldn't live, work, or study easily. In Austria, Jews may have lived in ghettos, but new doors were open to them. Meitner's father was one of the first Jews to become a lawyer in this more accepting world.

More accepting for Jewish men, at least. Going to college, following a profession, that was for sons, not daughters.

Still, Meitner learned however she could. She studied the

colors in a drop of oil. She noticed the reflections in puddles. She couldn't stop herself from asking questions about how the world worked. What made the film on the top of the puddle? How did light reflect off it? How could a drop of water be divided? What kept the drop together in the first place? She was "excited that there were such things to find out about in our world," she wrote later when thinking about her childhood.

To get the answers, Meitner wanted to go to high school. This was something girls simply didn't do in most of Europe in the late nineteenth century. Why bother to teach girls anything when they only needed to know how to raise children and run a household? In Vienna, not only were girls considered incapable of learning, but their presence would be a distraction for the boys. The University of Vienna declared that "the character of the university would be lost and the institution endangered by their [women's] presence."

Meitner didn't think she would distract anyone. Nobody would ever call her pretty. Not that she cared about that, since she didn't want a husband anyway. She just wanted to learn the way her brothers did.

Meitner's parents encouraged her. Her mother urged her to study on her own, saying, "Listen to your father and me, but think for yourself." Her father used himself as an example for his daughter, saying that if he could become a lawyer, then she could learn whatever she wanted. And like her father, she was lucky. In 1897, when Meitner was nineteen, the law in Austria changed and women were allowed to go to universities. But first they had to pass the difficult high school exit exam—without having actually gone to high school.

Her older sister Gisela started preparing for the test first, but Meitner quickly joined her. They studied Greek, Latin, math, physics, botany, zoology, mineralogy, psychology, logic, literature, and history. They read constantly, from as soon as they opened their eyes in the morning until they closed them, exhausted, at night. Meitner's younger brothers and sisters teased her that she would fail because "you've just walked across the room without picking up a book." Meitner was obsessive. This was her chance, and she wasn't going to miss it.

Gisela passed the difficult exam first and started medical school. As Meitner finished her studies, her father discouraged his younger daughter from following the same path—having two daughters in the impossibly male field of medicine was too much. Medicine wasn't Meitner's passion anyway. Physics was. She wanted to figure out how the world worked, but she didn't think physics had any practical applications. Medicine seemed the more noble, useful thing to do.

So it was a relief when Meitner's father urged her to follow her real interest. He knew any profession would be difficult for a young woman. To face the many obstacles, you had to care deeply about your subject, be willing to fight constantly for your right to be in that field. The tough high school exit exam was only the first hurdle.

TWO

EDUCATION AT LAST!

Of the fourteen young women who dared take the test, Meitner was one of four who passed. Starting at the University of Vienna in 1901, she decided to follow her heart and study physics.

She felt totally out of place, too terrified to say a word. She'd never gone to school with boys, never had to speak up.

Many professors didn't welcome the new women.

The man who taught most of Meitner's classes did. Ludwig Boltzmann's own daughter was a fellow student.

In his courses, Meitner felt accepted. Even more important, Boltzmann was a brilliant physicist and teacher.

Meitner called Boltzmann's lectures "the most beautiful and stimulating that I have ever heard . . . He himself was so enthusiastic about everything he taught us that one left every lecture with the feeling that a completely new and wonderful world had been revealed." Boltzmann's big bushy beard shook as he spoke, his thundering voice commanding his students' attention. And what he taught was fascinating. Boltzmann was an early believer in atoms, which many established physicists mocked. Could you see an atom? How could you believe in something that was invisible? The controversy Boltzmann described made clear to Meitner that science pretended to be objective but was often shaped by human bias. Meitner wanted to follow Boltzmann's path—she was hungry to discover what she didn't know, not look for confirmation of how she wanted things to be.

Boltzmann recognized Meitner's talent. Her mind was quick, her work thorough and careful. She had an uncanny ability to see both the forest *and* the trees. Boltzmann advised her to go to graduate school. As her nephew later observed, "Boltzmann gave her the vision of physics as a battle for ultimate truth." Meitner wanted to fight that battle.

THREE

A PROFESSOR WITH NO PROFESSION

Meitner's first victory came when she got her doctorate from the University of Vienna, the second female PhD, the first in physics. But despite the impressive degree, nobody wanted to work with a woman. Even Marie Curie turned her down.

So she built her own equipment at home, figuring out how to make the tools she needed, as all physicists did then.

Once her "lab" was set up, she felt a thrill of accomplishment. Now she could spend long hours exploring things much smaller than water droplets, things nobody could see.

Meitner focused on the new science of radioactivity, measuring the absorption of alpha and beta radiation in different metals. This was cutting-edge work, the kind Marie Curie was doing in Paris.

Working by herself, Meitner figured out a way to measure the scattering of alpha particles. Her results were important enough to publish in a scientific journal in 1907, when she was just twenty-eight. But even with that boost to her reputation, there was no future for a woman physicist in Vienna. Everyone told her the same thing: Go to Berlin. That was where all the important work in physics was happening. In Berlin, she'd get to know some of the greatest physicists of the time.

She had already met a professor from Berlin, Max Planck, when he'd come to lecture in Vienna. Like her, he was working on radioactivity. Planck wasn't an inspiring speaker, but his work was fascinating. He focused on quantum physics, a new field with exciting implications. That was enough for Meitner to decide to go to Berlin as everyone suggested. Her father, as always, supported her: "I admire your courage." He offered a small allowance until she could find a paid position. She also earned money writing and translating articles for science magazines under the name L. Meitner—never Lise Meitner.

Impressed with the work of L. Meitner, *Brockhaus Ency-*

clopedia approached her about writing a piece on radioactivity. Meitner hoped this would be the start of regular paying work for them, but when they realized L. was for Lise, they quickly took back the offer. They "would not think of printing an article written by a woman!"

Meitner continued to write articles, though never for the *Encyclopedia*, continued to sign her work "L. Meitner," continued to get by on the small sums she earned this way, along with the allowance from her father. At least she could disguise herself in writing by using her initial rather than her full name. She had worse problems at the University of Berlin, where everyone could see she wasn't a man.

Berlin in 1907 may have been ahead of Vienna in terms of science, but it was behind in how the city treated women. Germany still did not allow women as university students and would not officially open doors to them until the following summer, 1908. Meitner had no idea of this when she first walked onto campus, but it quickly became clear that the University of Berlin was entirely male, professors and students. Meitner wasn't even five feet tall and was easily cowed. She thought she was used to being the odd woman student, but Berlin was scarier than Vienna, the glares of the men more cutting. Meitner felt like such an outsider, so completely unwelcome, that her natural shyness turned into "bordering on fear of people." She was terrified that she simply didn't belong: "Women's education was just beginning to develop . . . I was very uneasy in my mind as to whether I would be able to become a scientist."

As she hesitated over whether to dare enter the university building, a former palace with an impressive colonnade, she saw another woman walking across the campus. Gerta von Ubisch was a physics student who had convinced professors to allow her to audit classes. She couldn't get a degree, but she could learn. She suggested that Meitner do the same. That little bit of encouragement was all Meitner needed. She wasn't the only woman student, no matter how alien she felt.

Meitner went first to see Max Planck for permission to sit in on his lectures. His droopy mustache, shiny bald head, and narrow eyes made his face look more stern than welcoming. But his words were gentle.

"He received me very kindly and soon afterwards invited me to his home. The first time I visited him there he said to me, 'But you are a Doctor already! What more do you want?' When I replied that I would like to gain some real understanding of physics, he just said a few friendly words and did not pursue the matter any further. Naturally, I concluded that he could have no very high opinion of women students, and possibly that was true enough at the time."

In fact, Planck's opinion of female scholars had been published a decade earlier by a Berlin journalist who asked one hundred professors what they thought about women in academia. Some strongly supported allowing women access. They believed that "keeping women from universities is an injustice that has gone on far too long." Others were passionately opposed, considering women a threat to the educational mission of universities: Classes would have to be on a lower level if women with their limited intelligence were allowed to attend. Planck didn't go that far, but he doubted that women could be good students. It was, he argued, against their very "nature," though he admitted there might be a freak "Amazon," the rare case of a woman capable of understanding science.

Did Planck consider Meitner one of these strange exceptions? He certainly encouraged her, the only woman he supported that way. But Planck wasn't the only barrier Meitner faced. She needed a place to do experimental work. So she screwed up her courage to ask Professor Heinrich Rubens, the head of the experimental physics institute, for a lab where she could continue her research.

Rubens suggested she could be his unpaid assistant, helping

with his experiments. But Meitner wanted to follow her own interests, to run her own experiments. She was trying to figure out how to politely refuse when Rubens mentioned that a young chemist, Dr. Otto Hahn, was interested in collaborating with Meitner. He'd heard of her work in radioactivity and read her one published article. Just then, Hahn himself came into Rubens's office. It was a lucky coincidence for Meitner. And for Hahn.

FOUR

A PARTNERSHIP BETTER THAN MARRIAGE

Hahn and Meitner were the same age, and his easygoing manner immediately set her at ease. Like Meitner, Hahn was working on radioactivity. Most importantly, he wasn't pompous or rigid, overbearing or bossy.

Hahn wasn't put off by Meitner being a woman. The other chemists at the institute had no idea what he was doing. Radioactivity was such a new field, and no scientists in Berlin were working on it. Only Meitner and Hahn. He felt lucky to have found her.

Hahn was charming and sociable, everything Meitner wasn't. And he was ambitious. He knew that to work on radiation, he needed a physicist to clarify and interpret the experiments he wanted to do.

Meitner was smart, a physicist up on the latest in radioactivity. Hahn felt he could rely on her.

And Meitner thought she could trust him. He didn't bark orders at her or treat her like a servant. In fact, he didn't treat her like a woman at all, neither with scorn nor with flirtation. He treated her like a physicist. That made him the perfect partner. That fall day in 1907, they started a collaboration that would last more than thirty years.

Rubens agreed to the arrangement. There was just one problem: Women weren't allowed inside the Chemistry Institute. Their long hair was a fire hazard, and that was that. Determined to work with someone who actually knew something about radioactivity, Hahn pressed for a compromise. Meitner's hair, after all, was tightly held in a bun. He kept nagging until Meitner was offered a room in the basement where she could work by herself. She could never go upstairs to the official labs where the men worked, but she could clear out an old carpenter's shop and make her own equipment. She would have to use a separate side entrance and run down the street to use the bathroom at a nearby restaurant or hotel. And, of course, she would hold no official position and would not be paid. Hahn saw this as a huge victory.

Meitner jumped at the offer. A lab of her own was all she wanted! She could continue scraping by on her meager allowance and translation work. And even if the "real" labs were off-limits, she was allowed to attend the meetings where the researchers (all men) talked about current projects, presented findings, and shared discoveries. She would be part of a world of scientists. That was all that mattered.

At these regular Wednesday physics colloquia, Meitner met a host of impressive young physicists. Many became good friends. "This group of young physicists made up an unusual circle," she wrote. "Not only were they brilliant scientists—five of them later received the Nobel Prize—they were also exceptionally nice people to know. Each was ready to help the other, each welcomed the other's success. You can understand what it meant to me to be received in such a friendly manner into this circle." At these meetings, Meitner was a fellow physicist, exploring how the world worked, like everyone else. The University of Berlin even introduced her to a couple of women scientists, Eva von Bahr and Elizabeth Schiemann. At both the institute and the university, Meitner made friendships that would last a lifetime, something she had never expected.

When women were officially allowed into the university and the institute the following year, a ladies' room was installed, saving Meitner the walk down the street to find a bathroom. And Meitner was finally allowed access to the official labs, though she still stayed in the basement for her own research. She had no paid position, but alone in her makeshift lab with her jerry-rigged equipment, Meitner felt part of a bigger world. The doors to physics had opened a crack for her, and she was determined to stride through. She would discover the truths Boltzmann had promised she would find.

FIVE

THE NEW SCIENCE OF RADIOACTIVITY

These were early days in radioactivity research. Neither Meitner nor Hahn took any precautions handling their materials. Radioactive elements arrived in cardboard boxes and were touched with bare hands.

They got constant headaches and occasional burns but considered it all normal.

Marie Curie, who received two Nobel Prizes for her work on radioactivity, carried test tubes of radium in her pockets.

She eventually died from radiation poisoning.

Meitner didn't know to be worried about that. She was excited to work on beta particles with Hahn.

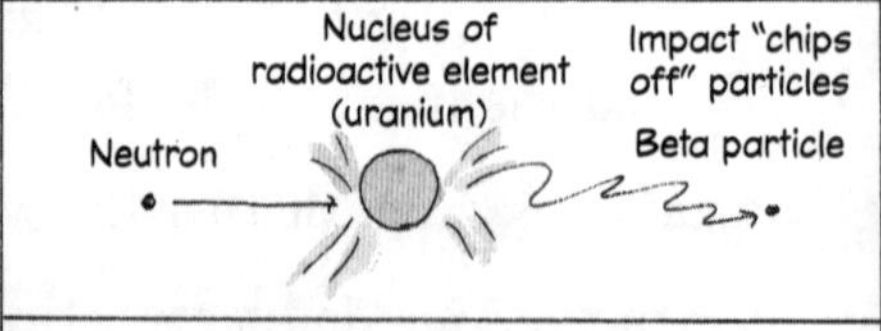
Nucleus of radioactive element (uranium)
Impact "chips off" particles
Neutron
Beta particle

Scientists had only recently accepted the idea that the atom existed. Radiation science looked at changes in the atom.

Physicists were bombarding the element uranium with particles and reporting the results. They thought they were discovering new elements by "chipping away" at the nucleus. They had no idea how wrong they were, though Meitner would be the one to figure out what was really happening. Until then, there was a race to find as many new elements as possible.

Hahn and Meitner worked closely together but were careful to maintain a distance. Hahn, already married, never treated Meitner like a woman. Nor was she like his male colleagues. She was in her own category, the Amazon described by Planck, a total exception to normal women. Hahn later wrote:

> *There was no question of any closer relationship between us outside the laboratory. Lise Meitner had had a strict, lady-like upbringing and was very reserved, even shy . . . For many years I never had a meal with Lise Meitner except on official occasions. Nor did we ever go for a walk together. Apart from the physics colloquia that we attended, we met only in the carpenter's shop. There we generally worked until nearly eight in the evening, so that one or the other of us would have to go out to buy salami or cheese before the shops shut at that hour. We never ate our cold supper together there. Lise Meitner went home alone, and so did I. And yet we were really very close friends.*

Careful lines were drawn by both of them. Meitner, because she wanted to be seen as a scientist, not a woman. Hahn, because Meitner wasn't someone you could joke with, not someone for small talk. Her friends admired her for her intelligence, her focus, her dedication to physics. There was no other side to her. Without science, she felt she had no identity. For her, Hahn provided exactly the kind of partner she needed. He was someone she could talk to endlessly about their work, someone who understood the implications of radioactive decay, someone who got excited about beta particles.

They worked together so closely for so long, their relationship became a kind of work marriage. Through the years, Meitner wrote some of her most personal letters to Hahn. And Hahn wrote about family and work worries, while relying heavily on Meitner to interpret their research. Without her, he was half a scientist, an experimenter without the ability to read the meaning behind the results. He understood the outcomes only in terms of chemistry, able to identify the elements and particles that occurred. He had no idea what was happening within the atomic nucleus, what caused the "new" elements and particles—that was a question of physics. Without Hahn, Meitner wouldn't have been able to run as many experiments. And his name alongside hers on their published papers gave her instant authority. As in a marriage, there was important work done together that would have been impossible by themselves. And as in a marriage, the eventual divorce was messy and complicated, an ending that wasn't an ending.

Hahn became a professor. Meitner remained an unpaid assistant, still scraping by through translating scientific articles from English to German. Meitner was an expert at living cheaply, eating little, and spending next to nothing on clothes. After all, she had no needs beyond a lab. If she'd been forced to sleep there, she would have.

With Hahn, she published numerous articles on beta radiation. They published three major papers in 1908, six in 1909, and fourteen in the next three years. Hahn, in his official lab, ran the experiments. Meitner interpreted the results and wrote the articles. Together they discovered new radioactive elements, expanding the understanding of radioactivity.

Their work got so much attention that when the new Kaiser Wilhelm Institute (KWI) was built and the chemistry and physics departments separated, each of them was given a modern new lab, fitted out with protective cases for anything radioactive and clean surfaces to prevent contamination from previous experiments. They now worked in healthier places. The frequent headaches they'd had before disappeared. Most importantly, at age thirty, Meitner was appointed scientific associate, an actual title with a real, though tiny, salary.

Meitner had always thought of herself as one thing only—a physicist. "I love physics with all my heart . . . It is a kind of personal love, as one has for a person to whom one is grateful for many things." Meitner's world was in the lab. And now that lab was light-filled, clean, and airy. The days of the dark basement were over.

SIX

OUT OF THE DARK

When Ernest Rutherford received the 1908 Nobel Prize in Chemistry, he stopped by the KWI to visit the famous team of Hahn and Meitner.
Doctor Meitner, may I introduce you to Doctor Rutherford? I worked with him in Cambridge as his assistant.
Herr Doctor, this is Miss Doctor Meitner, the physicist I work with.
Oh, I thought you were a man!
Meitner was used to this. In fact, usually she was simply ignored. People at the lab would pointedly say hello to Hahn and treat her as if she were invisible.
At least she could live on her small salary. And she had Hahn as a male face to present their work at departmental meetings.
Still, she felt like she didn't really belong.
"Sometimes I lack courage, and then my life, with its great insecurity, the constantly repeated worries, the feeling of being an exception, the absolute aloneness, seems almost unbearable to me."
She had women friends she wrote to often, but none were physicists like her. She had kept going when they had given up.

Meitner could do physics experiments, could go to conferences, and was constantly learning new things and meeting fascinating scientists, like Albert Einstein, who at thirty-one was the same age and already famous. They first met in 1909, when they lectured at a conference in Salzburg, Austria. Meitner was there with other physicists from the KWI. They had all come to hear Einstein, the young patent office clerk with exciting new theories. Meitner presented first. She was, as usual, the only woman speaking. Her topic was new groups of beta emitters in radium series. She calmed her nerves and spoke clearly and passionately, the way she remembered Boltzmann's lectures, her love of physics conquering her shyness. Einstein, sitting in the front row, applauded enthusiastically. Meitner's face lit up with a rare smile.

Einstein had just quit his day job as a patent clerk in Bern, Switzerland, and this was his first invitation to lecture. He spoke as if he were having a conversation with friends (very smart friends). He described his ideas on the nature of motion, how all motion in the universe is relative except the speed of light. He gave the everyday example of how when we're sitting in a train at the station and another train passes by, we have the feeling that the car we're in is moving, though we're sitting still. Weight is also relative, dependent on speed. In another example from daily life, Einstein described how a child running full tilt into a person feels heavier than their actual weight–forty pounds feels like one hundred pounds on forceful impact. He said, "One should think of matter as condensed energy."

Meitner had spoken about experiments and results. Einstein spoke about theories. His second lecture described how mass is a form of energy (and vice versa), as derived from the equation that would become internationally famous. "Since the velocity of light is a huge quantity, a small amount of mass–multiplied by the square of the velocity–is equivalent to a very large amount of energy. Thus, if *m* stands for Matter, *e* for Energy and the speed of light *c* . . . $E=mc^2$." This was the first time Einstein presented the equation that has become synonymous with his name. The response was a smattering of applause. Nobody quite grasped the meaning of his words, what his simple-sounding theory meant.

Meitner wrote, "I almost understood him!" She did grasp some things: "At that time I certainly did not yet realize the full implications of his theory of relativity and the way in which it would contribute to a revolutionary transformation of our concepts of time and space. In the course of this lecture he did, however, take the theory of relativity and . . . showed that to every radiation must be attributed an inert mass. These two facts were so overwhelmingly new and surprising that, to this day, I remember the lecture well." She would in fact remember the ideas when she needed them most, to make her own major discovery.

After the talk, physicists asked Einstein to explain further. Did he mean that mass held energy the way a lump of coal burns off heat? No, Einstein clarified, he was thinking about the atomic level of things, that if you could reach inside the core of an atom, an immense amount of energy could be released. But since the atomic core, the nucleus, was indivisible, such power was only theoretical. Like many others, Meitner agreed with Einstein. There was the potential for enormous energy inside the atom but no way to harness it. It would stay locked inside the atom forever.

In 1913, Planck brought Einstein to work in Berlin at the KWI. Now Meitner could talk with him at the weekly meetings. The year before, Planck had offered Meitner her first paid teaching position at the University of Berlin—not as a professor but as Planck's assistant at his Institute of Theoretical Physics. By then, she had an international reputation for her research on radioactivity, but the only teaching job she could get was grading exams and papers for someone else. Planck wanted to offer her a full professorship, but no woman had ever held that title. It was already revolutionary having a woman as an assistant.

She later wrote, "Not only did this give me a chance to work under such a wonderful man and eminent scientist as Planck, it was also the entrance to my scientific career. It was the passport to scientific activity in the eyes of most scientists and a great help to overcoming many current prejudices against academic women."

Meitner now had a heavy academic load, grading sometimes more than two hundred assignments a week, all while doing her own research, continuing to present at the Wednesday colloquia, and publishing papers. None of it felt like a burden. Just the opposite—she was excited, happy. And determined to make her own important discovery one day.

SEVEN

WAR AND SCIENCE

1914: Besides the work at the University of Berlin, Planck got Meitner a paid position at the KWI as a "guest physicist," the best title he could offer. At last, Meitner hoped to be taken seriously. But something much bigger than being a woman got in the way: war.
Germany declares war!
Read all about it!
War? What does that mean for the institute? For science?
July 28, 1914: Tensions simmering in the Balkans lit a spark that set Germany, Austria-Hungary, and the Ottoman Empire in a war against Russia, Serbia, France, and Britain, among other countries on both sides. Millions of men would fight in this "Great War," a war started without clear reasons or goals but one that dragged in most of the world.
Hahn was drafted and went off to serve in the infantry.
His expertise soon placed him in a special unit.
Meitner volunteered as a nurse in the X-ray unit in the Austrian army. She was posted to the Russian front. It was chaotic and dangerous, nothing like her quiet lab.

As a specialist, Meitner was treated like a doctor rather than a nurse, a mark of respect that was new to her after her experience in the world of science. Maybe a medical career wouldn't have been so tough after all, she thought, remembering her father's warning that only an exceptional woman could succeed as a doctor.

It was too late to change careers. Besides, she was a physicist through and through. Seeing the practical uses for radiation in X-rays only inspired her more to get back to her research. Much as she wanted to help the wounded men, being away from the lab tore at her very sense of self. As she wrote to Hahn on October 14, 1915:

"You can hardly imagine my way of life. That physics exists, that I once worked in physics and one day will again, seems as far away to me now as if had never happened, nor will again."

Hahn didn't write such forlorn letters. He had been moved from the infantry to a special unit and was still working in his chosen field, chemistry. In fact, he was helping the German military develop chemical weapons, poison gas to use on enemy soldiers, under the direction of Fritz Haber, a renowned chemist who was the president of the KWI for Physical Chemistry and Electrochemistry. Haber and Einstein were close friends until the war erupted. Einstein was a staunch pacifist. "Warfare," he said, "cannot be humanized. It can only be abolished." Haber disagreed. He thought chemical warfare was more "humane," since it would shorten the war.

Hahn was part of this "humane" effort. He was posted to the 126th Infantry Regiment in Flanders, the northern region of Belgium, where he prepared the first gas attack of the war, using chlorine. At the last minute, the commanders decided to use the gas on a different Belgian town, Ypres, sparing Hahn from being responsible for its first direct use in the war. Haber himself oversaw the release of 5,700 gas cylinders, throwing up 167 tons of chlorine into the long-awaited wind. Within minutes, the chlorine cloud had wounded 5,000 men. An inherently inaccurate weapon since the wind could change at any moment, this first test also killed 1,000 German soldiers. Still, the military considered it a success, and they tried again two days later, this time wounding 10,000 soldiers and killing 4,000. The *New York Times* reported the disaster on April 25, 1915:

"Some got away in time, but many, alas, not understanding

the new danger were not so fortunate and were overcome by the fumes and died poisoned. Among those who escaped, nearly all cough and spit blood, the chlorine attacking the mucous membrane. The dead were turned black at once . . . [The Germans] made no prisoners. Whenever they saw a soldier whom the fumes had not quite killed, they snatched away his rifle . . . and advised him to lie down 'to die better.'"

Hahn was given his chance to supervise chemical weapons in Galicia (then part of Austria, now in Ukraine), using both chlorine and phosgene gas on enemy soldiers. Almost 1,500 men worked in his unit to develop these weapons. There were serious accidents, even deaths, among his own men while testing the gases, but Hahn had no qualms about what he was doing. He told himself that the French and British were doing the same thing, so the only solution was to make better, more powerful weapons first. Besides, he reasoned, scientists must do their best work. It wasn't their job to figure out how things got used—that was a military decision. Haber agreed, arguing that if a scientist had any moral responsibility, it was toward his own country, not toward mankind in general. This was the first war in which science was an active participant. But it was not the last.

Hahn's contribution was important, but the real "father of

chemical warfare" was Haber. In his forties, Haber was too old for regular military service and, because he was Jewish, was ineligible for an officer's position (the usual place for someone of his expertise). As a staunchly patriotic German, he offered to do research on toxic gases. Besides weaponizing chlorine, Haber developed a method to make ammonia artificially from nitrogen and hydrogen gases, allowing Germany to continue to produce fertilizer and fertilizer-based explosives during the war despite trade embargoes. It was Haber who invented mustard gas, the chemical cloud that burned—and killed—tens of thousands of soldiers on both sides. And Haber who showed his country how to make highly toxic chemicals from simple, widely available ingredients.

Haber's chemical weapons led to the deaths of 92,000 soldiers on both sides and the injury of 1.3 million. After the war, his name appeared on a list of alleged war criminals. Haber fled to Switzerland until the Allies dropped the charges (possibly because of their own use of chemical weapons). His name cleared, Haber went back to the KWI in Berlin.

After World War I, an interviewer asked Hahn about his experiences with toxins: "You have told us that you several times saw with your own eyes the effect of poison gases on enemy soldiers."

That was true, Hahn answered, admitting to being "ashamed" and "very much upset." At least, at first. He continued to work on lethal gases, with the German company IG Farben funding his later research at the KWI.

At the end of his life, Hahn explained away his part in chemical warfare: "As a result of continuous work with these highly toxic substances, our minds were so numbed that we no longer had any scruples about the whole thing. Anyway, our enemies had by now adopted our methods . . . We were no longer exclusively the aggressors but found ourselves more and more on the receiving end."

Meitner, however, wasn't numb. She was deeply disturbed that science was being used for military purposes. She didn't confront Hahn about the murderous chemicals. She understood he was following orders. Instead, she avoided the subject entirely in her letters. But she was horrified to see science used for evil rather than for pure knowledge, for the good of humanity. After she heard about Hahn's work in the summer of 1916, she applied for a release from military service. After all, she didn't even understand why the war was being fought. The whole world was fighting, and nobody seemed to know why except the generals. She saw how the military and companies like IG Farben were directing research at the KWI. She saw how they were using scientists like Hahn. She couldn't stop him personally, but she hoped that once back in the lab, she could shape policy and prevent the KWI from becoming a tool for war instead of a place for pure scientific discovery. She thought she could make a bigger difference fighting the weaponization of science than helping wounded soldiers. She could scarcely have imagined that her own discovery would lead to the deadliest weapon of them all.

EIGHT

BACK IN THE LAB

Despite the war, Meitner and Hahn continued to collaborate through letters. They were looking for the origin of the element actinium and eventually discovered a new heavy element, protactinium, which decayed (or turned into) actinium. Meitner did the experiments, discussed the results with Hahn, wrote up their findings, and published them.

It was her work, her interpretations, but she always included his name.

So Hahn got the credit for their discovery of a new isotope of protactinium. The Association of German Chemists awarded Hahn the Emil Fischer Medal for this groundbreaking work.

Congratulations!
Thank you.

For you!

They gave Meitner a copy of Hahn's medal.

Hahn didn't object to the fake medal for Meitner, but he was still a perfect partner in many ways. So after Germany's defeat in the war, Hahn and Meitner returned to collaborating in person just as before. But things were very different outside the walls of the lab. The surrender terms imposed on Germany were so crushing that after the government paid reparations to France and Britain, the nation was effectively broke. To continue to operate, the easy solution was to print more and more money. Inflation soared so that by early 1923, the German mark, once valued at 75 marks to the dollar, was worth 18,000 to the dollar. By midyear, it took more than 4.5 million marks to equal one US dollar. By the fall of 1923, a loaf of bread cost 200,000,000,000 marks!

Times were tough for everyone, but Meitner wasn't paying attention to food. Her reputation shone brighter than ever thanks to all the papers she'd been publishing throughout the war. By herself, she was doing major work on beta and gamma radiation, proving that after beta decay, secondary radiation—gamma radiation—was released, a chain effect of radiation. Radioactive substances aren't stable. Instead, they decay until they reach a stable state. This decay doesn't take the form of rotting away like an apple core. It's a change at the atomic level as positrons–electrons with a positive charge–are lost until the atomic structure reaches a state it can stay in. Meitner was looking at this decay chain of radioactive substances. Besides the papers she published with Hahn, she published ten of her own immediately after the war. It was a spurt of productivity, a time when she felt secure in her work–until everything changed.

NINE

AFTER THE WAR

1918: Germany struggled to recover from the war. There was political and economic upheaval.
I'd like to present a finding on radioactive processes today.
To Meitner, all that mattered was that scientists were back in their labs. She could speak at the regular Wednesday meeting.
Fascinating talk.
Very interesting.
You were both eloquent and clear. I'm curious to see where this line of research takes you.
Max Planck, president of the Kaiser Wilhelm Society
Heinrich Rubens, director of the KWI
Albert Einstein, young physicist on the rise
Their praise was just what Meitner needed.
Who cared if food was scarce and prices had skyrocketed? Meitner was being taken seriously as a scientist!

Meitner wrote to her family in Vienna: "There really is enough to eat, although the prices are completely crazy; a kilogram of margarine costs 30–40 million, one egg costs 1½–2 million . . . Personally I feel fine . . . I myself don't mind if there is less to eat. It's much worse for ill people and children—no milk, hardly any butter."

With such high prices and the currency worth so little, people had to take wheelbarrows full of cash to buy groceries. Meitner tried to reassure her mother—who sent packets of coffee, sometimes a cake—that she was better off than most. She didn't have a family to worry about. Besides, she was used to living on a tight budget, eating little. It was much harder for Hahn, with a young son. She saw him pick up his pay from the university cashier in a suitcase, the large pile of money worth so little. Meitner, with her lower salary, could stash her meager pay in her purse, not enough to buy even a single egg.

As bad as things were in general, for Meitner things were going well. She was now considered the female spokesperson for quantum physics (not that there were any other women for the role—her old schoolfriend Gerta von Ubisch had dropped out of physics long ago). With Hahn, she showed how uranium decay could be used to estimate the age of the earth, and then the sun, leading to follow-up work suggesting that the sun was powered by the conversion of mass to energy.

Other discoveries included an improved measure for the mass of a neutron. Meitner also observed that even (rather than odd) atomic numbers tend to be more stable, that is, to undergo less radioactive decay. These were all important contributions, any one of which would have brought her fame. Together, they made her reputation truly stellar.

Like most physicists of the time, Meitner continued to build her own equipment from things that could be found in a hardware or housewares store: rubber tubing, beakers, glass piping, wire mesh. Bigger machines like cyclotrons, which were used to study particles' behavior, were just beginning to be developed. In the 1920s, Meitner was one of the first physicists to use a new piece of equipment, a cloud chamber. She built her own from a small aquarium. The movement of different particles showed up as tracks in the mist (the water or alcohol cloud created inside the chamber). These different tracks could then be captured on film.

These were the years when scientists were redefining atomic structure, making new, exciting discoveries about what was inside an atom, how it all held together. Meitner was convinced she had her own contribution to make. She wasn't sure what it would be, but she was determined to see clearly inside the mysterious workings of the nucleus. What she found would change the world forever.

TEN

A PROFESSOR AT LAST

A cloud chamber is a sealed glass box that allows physicists to "see" particles.

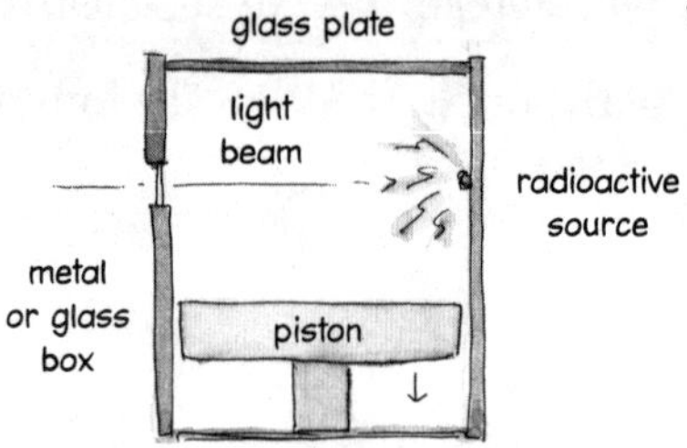
glass plate
light beam
radioactive source
metal or glass box
piston

traces of particles captured by a cloud chamber

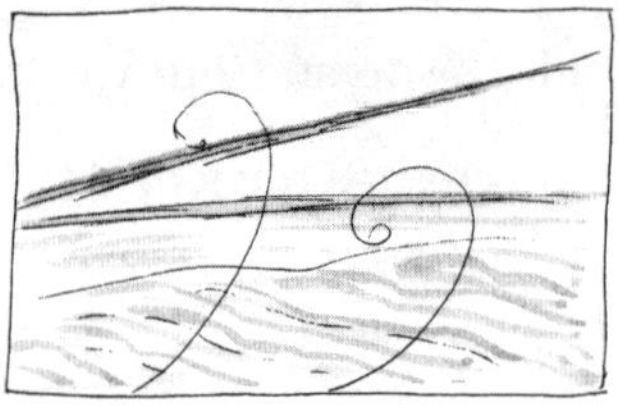

radioactive patterns for Meitner to interpret

The radioactive particles leave a trail when interacting with water or alcohol vapor. These tracks have characteristic shapes: An alpha particle leaves a thick, straight line; an electron's path is wispy; and a cosmic ray leaves yet another kind of mark. The cloud chamber allowed a look at all of them.

With all this new information, the model of the atom was changing. What was it really like?

1904: Plum pudding model

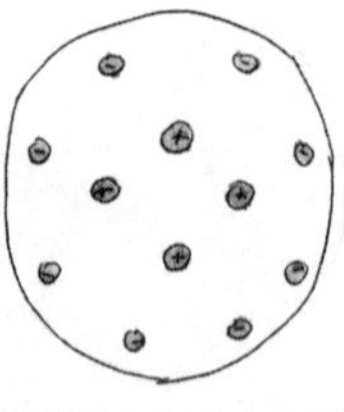

The British physicist J. J. Thomson described the interior of the atom as dotted with electrons, like raisins in a pudding.

1911: Rutherford's model

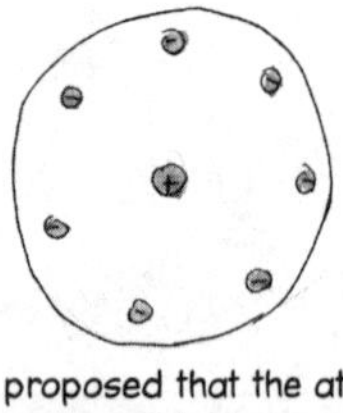

Rutherford proposed that the atom was mostly empty space with electrons orbiting a fixed, positively charged nucleus. Gravity held the electrons in their orbit. If the atom were the size of a cathedral, the nucleus would be a tiny fly in its center, with *lots* of empty space around.

1913: Niels Bohr's model

Bohr expanded on Rutherford's model, with orbits similar to the planets and electrons held to their orbits by electrostatic forces, not gravity.

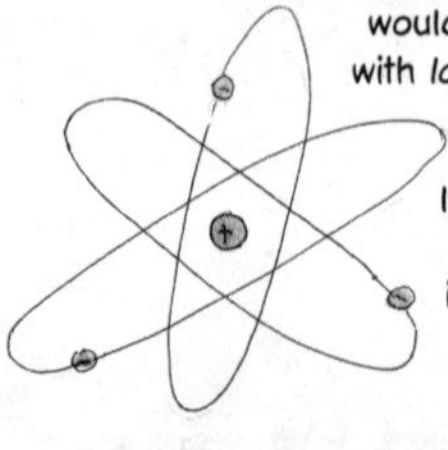

If gravity were the force keeping the electrons in orbit, the atom would collapse into itself. It wouldn't be stable.

In 1920, Meitner published ten articles on subjects like radioactive processes and cosmic rays. For the first time, she didn't feel totally reliant on Hahn, though they still worked together. She had her own reputation now, her own body of work. Perhaps she would finally get the position she deserved.

Impressed by Meitner's work, a university in Prague offered her just what she wanted, a full academic title. There was hyperinflation in Germany and there had been military attempts to seize control of the government, but Meitner hesitated to leave the KWI, her home for many years. She asked Planck for his advice.

Planck wanted Meitner to stay, but he could hardly ask her to continue as an assistant in Berlin when a full professorship awaited her elsewhere. So he did what academics always do—used an outside offer to create a better position at home. Planck persuaded the KWI to promote Meitner, rather than risk losing an internationally recognized scientist. Meitner would finally be a professor, the first for a woman in Germany! She would be paid only a third of Hahn's salary, but for her, the 1,000 marks a year were a fortune after years of making hardly anything. Meitner quickly agreed.

Normally, to gain such a title, a thesis had to be submitted and accepted. Since Meitner had already published so much and made important discoveries, the university waived that requirement. But Meitner still had to pass an oral exam, given by Max von Laue and Heinrich Rubens.

Rubens, despite his previous concern about women in science, admitted that Meitner was at the top of her field. Laue had long been a friend as well as a colleague. He admired her work and the clarity of her writing. The oral exam became a chat about Meitner's research. After all, she could have given *them* the exam!

As *Professor* Meitner, she gave her first university lecture: "The Significance of Radioactivity for Cosmic Processes." The Berlin academic press reported the talk as being on "cosmetic" rather than "cosmic" processes. After all, women were more likely to discuss makeup than the universe. Meitner didn't ask for a correction. She worried that making a fuss would make her seem like a temperamental woman, when she didn't want to be seen as a woman at all.

Meitner wrote that "life need not be easy provided only it was not empty. And this wish I have been granted." She had her work, her colleagues, her friends (who were her colleagues), and the occasional concert as a break from physics. Nothing else mattered.

Also in 1920, the Danish physicist Niels Bohr came to lecture in Berlin. Meitner went with friends to hear him. Bohr gave a talk on his "correspondence principle," about the importance of a series of spectral lines and their interpretation. Meitner wrote that "when James Franck, Gustav Hertz, and I came out of the lecture, we were somewhat depressed because we had the feeling that we had understood very little."

The younger scientists wanted to get Bohr alone, away from the big shots, so they could have a quiet discussion with him all to themselves. Bohr was not yet forty, with a young, babyish face, but he was still intimidating. The three were huddled together, trying to figure out how they could possibly approach him, when the Danish physicist came up from behind the group. "Why not just ask me?" he suggested.

Relieved, the junior scientists set up a meeting at Haber's villa in Dahlem. They could talk while Haber was away at work. When they all got to the villa, they were met by an unexpected houseguest, Einstein. It was a distinguished group, the best in physics. Away from the crowd, Bohr explained everything clearly. Meitner told him of her own work on beta and gamma rays. Intrigued, he invited her to speak at the Institute for Theoretical Physics, in Copenhagen. It was the beginning of a long friendship.

The following year, Meitner took her first trip to Copenhagen, something that would become an annual tradition, staying with Bohr and his wife, Margrethe. There she met another German physicist, also a guest of the Bohrs, Werner Heisenberg. He had been an assistant to Bohr and was visiting while on his way to take up a teaching position. It was the first time Meitner heard him explain his uncertainty principle, about the inherent imprecision of measurements in physics, something that would win Heisenberg the Nobel Prize in 1932.

The discussions at the Copenhagen institute were exhilarating. Talking about quantum physics, about atomic structure, Meitner didn't feel like an outsider. She didn't feel suffocated by the overwhelming shyness that could still paralyze her in new situations. Instead, she felt she was at the very center of the most exciting new discoveries in physics.

Finally, it didn't matter that she was a woman!

But now, it mattered that she was Jewish.

ELEVEN

"JEWISH" PHYSICS VS. "ARYAN" PHYSICS

As early as the 1920s, the German scientific establishment saw Einstein's theories and quantum physics as a "Jewish fraud." There was wholesome Aryan (white) physics and then there was the evil Jewish version.

While Adolf Hitler was in prison in 1924 for a failed coup attempt, he wrote *Mein Kampf* (*My Struggle*) and took on the stature of a martyr. Two Nobel Prize winners wrote letters in support of Hitler and all he stood for.

We need lucid minds as scientists . . . just as Hitler is one. He and his comrades in the struggle appear to us as God's gifts from times of old when races were purer, people were greater, and minds less deluded.
This we feel; and these divine gifts should not be taken from us. This thought alone should be a solid enough basis to hold the nationally minded together toward their great goal: Founding a new Germany, with Hitler "beating the drum," in which the German spirit is . . . protected, nursed, and assisted so that it can then finally thrive again and develop . . . for the vindication of . . . life on our planet which is now dominated by an inferior (Jewish) spirit.
The enemy is Einstein — and any other Jewish physicist. They are the root of scientific perversion, OF EVIL!

In 1918, Max Planck, who was not Jewish, had won the Nobel Prize in Physics for the realization that light and electromagnetic waves were emitted in discrete packets of energy he called "quanta." These quanta weren't continuous, and Planck demonstrated that the very structure of energy is discontinuous and could only be changed in distinct increments. Scientists had thought of energy as continuous, like a stream of milk pouring into a cup of coffee. Planck showed that energy was more like cubes of sugar: You could add one, two, or more separate cubes.

Academic journals did all they could to discredit this cutting-edge science and the researchers who contributed to it. Germans like Planck who worked in the field were called "white Jews"–white (what the Germans called Aryan) people with Jewish sympathies. (Jews themselves were not considered white but an inferior race.) The result was a steep decline in the number of students studying both physics and math. What wholesome Aryan German citizen wanted to be associated with such depraved Jewish thinking?

The chorus of establishment voices against "decadent

Jewish physics" grew until Planck felt he had to make a public statement. What was at stake was the rigor of scientific thinking, the unbiased exploration of the world, truth itself. In his lecture, "Physics in Struggle for a Worldview," Planck insisted, "The scientific irrefutability and consistency of physics comprises the direct challenge of truthfulness and honesty. Justness is inseparable from devotion to truth." Why, he wondered, would the incredible scientific discoveries of Einstein be seen as bad? Why would understanding the qualities of light on an atomic level be considered perverse simply because the scientists working on the question were Jewish? How could truth be wrong?

Meitner had always liked Planck. She said he was one of those people who made a room feel better just by entering it. With this lecture, she admired him all the more. She had been drawn to physics long ago because she saw it as Truth. Her first professor, Boltzmann, caught in his own fights with scientists skeptical of the existence of atoms, had inspired her by saying, "Bring forward what is true, write it so that it is clear, defend it to your last breath!" She didn't understand how a theory could be attacked simply because it was proposed by someone who was Jewish. Was all her work about to be questioned because of her own Jewishness?

Meitner had good reason to worry. Railing against the Jews and the damage they were doing to society came out of a deep hatred for Jewish people. It also proved to be a convenient distraction from the upheavals of the German economy after the war. It was easier to blame the Jews for ruining the country than admit the government's own role in the problems. This was a strategy that had been used successfully by many countries and societies for thousands of years, scapegoating Jews for any problems they faced. The old hatred thrived in the miserable postwar conditions.

Meitner tried to stay focused on her work. After all, like many German Jews, she'd been baptized as an adult. It was hard enough getting a position as a woman. It would have been doubly difficult with the added stigma of being Jewish. And religion didn't matter to her. In her mind, Judaism was a remnant from her parents' generation, a legacy she could pick up or ignore. She chose to ignore it and hoped others would as well.

In 1924, Meitner won the Prussian Academy of Sciences' Silver Liebniz Medal, a first for a woman. The following year, she was awarded the Vienna Academy of Sciences' Ignaz Lieben Prize. Meitner's father was proud to see his daughter recognized by their home city, proof that women could be scientists. And three years later in 1928, Meitner received a new award from an American organization, the Association to Aid Women in Science. It was the first time the award was given, and it was meant to be a "Nobel Prize for Women," since the Swedish organization was notoriously blind to women's achievements. Meitner received the award jointly with the French chemist Pauline Ramart-Lucas. In addition, she and Hahn were nominated for the Nobel Prize, the first of many times for the pair.

After years of being on the edge of things, years of being the only woman in the room, Meitner was being recognized by her colleagues for her extraordinary work. Despite the rumblings against decadent Jewish physics, Meitner felt completely at home in Berlin. And the awards made her feel protected. Yes, she'd heard the anti-Semitic rants of Hitler, but like so many others, she didn't take him seriously. The man had used the decade since his release from jail to build a loyal following with his National Socialist German Workers' Party, a fascist group promoting a stronger Germany. Meitner thought the Nazis, as they were called, were too radical to hold real power. Yes, they were getting a lot of attention, but it would all pass. She never once considered leaving her home over stupid politics.

TWELVE

HITLER TAKES POWER

Then, in January 1933, Hitler was sworn in as chancellor of the Third Reich, a powerful position as head of government. A month later, a raging fire in the Reichstag, the German parliament building in Berlin, provided the perfect excuse for Hitler to impose martial law and grab more power. The Nazis claimed the fire was set by communists trying to overthrow the government.

Hitler said, "These sub-humans (communists) do not understand how the people stand at our side. In their mouse-holes, out of which they now want to come, of course they hear nothing of the cheering from the masses."

This accusation was never proved, though many were arrested. Clues suggested the Nazis themselves caused the blaze as an excuse to take over the country.

Hermann Göring, president of the Reichstag and high up in the Nazi party, was a key witness at the trial of the four accused communists. He was said to have boasted to a general about setting the fire himself.

The only one who really knows about the Reichstag fire is me, for I set fire to it!

And saying this, he slapped his thigh.

The Reichstag fire was the fuel Hitler needed to seize control of the country. Furious that only one of the five accused men was convicted, Hitler set up a new "People's Court" to try all serious crimes such as treason. This court, like the rest of the government, was firmly under Nazi control. "National security" became a heavy-handed excuse to impose oppressive measures. Mass arrests of supposed communists followed as Hitler warned in fiery language that they were trying to start a civil war and take over the country. The day after the fire, Hitler asked President Paul von Hindenburg to sign the Reichstag Fire Decree, under Article 48 of the Weimar Constitution. The decree suspended most civil liberties in Germany, including freedom of the press, the right to free association, and the privacy of mail and phone lines. These rights were not reinstated during the Nazi reign—due, of course, to national security. The decree was used to control the press, and the era of ugly propaganda began, spreading "news" of how the Jews and communists were trying to take over the world and had to be stopped.

At first Meitner didn't think Hitler's fury would touch her.

Einstein, who was in California when Hitler came to power, quickly understood the danger. In an interview on March 10, 1933, Einstein said: "As long as the possibility remains open to me, I will live only in a country in which political freedom, tolerance, and equality of all citizens before the law prevail. The freedom of oral and written expression of political conviction constitutes a part of political freedom; respect for the convictions of an individual a part of tolerance. These conditions are not fulfilled at present in Germany. There, those who have especially served the cause of international understanding are being persecuted." The German government insisted that Planck expel Einstein from the KWI and the Berlin Academy of Sciences. Einstein spared Planck the trouble, turning in his resignation before he could be thrown out. The Reich was furious. How dare Einstein quit when they were about to fire the traitor? All they could do was issue a blustery statement that the Berlin Academy had no regret over Einstein leaving, since the Jew was waging an "atrocity campaign against Germany." Meitner saw the reaction to Einstein as a bit of ugly bluster. She didn't think any other Jewish professors would be kicked out. It was just a lot of noise, a way for Hitler to grandstand and feel important.

It turned out to be much more than that.

THIRTEEN

BOYCOTT THE JEWS!

April 1, 1933: A day of Jewish boycott.

FIGHT THE JEWS!
JEWS HAVE DESTROYED GERMAN BUSINESSES!

Storm troopers, Hitler's personal army, occupied colleges, universities, and law courts, throwing out all Jewish professionals. Stores were placarded with ugly signs. Nobody protested. Instead, crowds cheered the actions. Only a few professors complained about their colleagues' treatment. After all, only the Jews suffered, and they deserved it. Patriotic Germans were protected, better off under Hitler.

Meitner was terrified. She had thought being a woman was a curse, but it was nothing compared to this.

Will I lose everything?
What will happen to me?

She described her fears to Hahn, hoping for advice.

Hahn was teaching at Cornell University in the United States for the spring semester.

You're overreacting.
All is fine.

Hahn was sure that newspapers were just trying to "sensationalize German persecution of the Jews." He was hopeful about Hitler's "New Germany." Things would be better than ever.

Maybe Hahn didn't know about Hitler's Law for the Restoration of the Professional Civil Service of April 7, 1933, which made it illegal to employ Jews in any government agency, including universities and research institutes. Or that shortly after he left for America, Nazi soldiers came to the KWI and every other university in Germany, writing down everyone's names, noting who was Jewish. Throughout the country, a picture of Hitler had to be displayed in every home, alongside a copy of his book, *Mein Kampf* (*My Struggle*).

Meitner wasn't reassured by Hahn. She turned to Haber for advice. She wanted to know if she should, if she could, stay in Germany. Jewish himself, he had no answers for her. Meitner had admitted to being Jewish when pressed to fill out the required form, but she hoped that being Austrian rather than German would offer her some protection. Haber had no idea if that was true. He was torn over whether to stay himself.

Leo Szilard, a Hungarian Jewish physicist, was scheduled to teach a course with Meitner that spring. When he heard about the new law, he chose to quit rather than be fired. Like Einstein, he was all too aware of the dangers Hitler brought. He left Berlin for England. Meitner, he warned, should do the same.

Jews were kicked out of their jobs. They weren't allowed to

go to school, to run a business, to go to movies or most stores. They couldn't ride public transportation or even drive their own cars. Meitner's Jewish friends, Hertz and Franck, were forced to quit their positions and decided, like Szilard, to leave the country. They had to leave behind their property and bank accounts, but at least they could still teach, do research, and be part of physics. They encouraged Meitner to go with them.

It was a jolt to watch so many friends leave, but Meitner spent more time at the KWI than ever, trying to avoid screaming headlines and loudspeakers spouting slogans of hate. Still, she wasn't blind. She watched as Nazi brownshirts stoked a bonfire of "undesirable" books, many written by Jewish authors, in front of the University of Berlin in May 1933. The next blow came when Fritz Haber resigned as director of the KWI rather than agree to fire all the other German Jewish scientists and staff. Although he should have been exempt from the anti-Jewish act given his highly commended service during the Great War, Haber was pressured until he left. He may have been "a competent scientist," said Bernhard Rust, the Prussian minister of education, but "he was Jewish and had stocked the [KWI] . . . largely with Jewish scientists, thus blocking the path to advancement for many promising German ['Aryan'] scientists."

The scientific community as a whole said and did nothing as some of its most esteemed members were stripped of their positions and assets. Some surely stayed quiet out of fear. Others out of passivity. Still others out of approval. With so many Jewish professors and researchers forced out, scientists who had trouble getting positions before now found many jobs open to them.

Terrified of starting over with nothing, of losing her lab, her world of physics, Meitner refused to follow her friends. "It was . . . my life's work, and it seemed too terribly hard to separate myself from it," she later wrote a friend. She would be the last Jewish scientist left in Berlin.

FOURTEEN

A TALK WITH HITLER ABOUT SCIENCE

Max Planck's first job as director of the KWI, taking over from Haber, was to make sure the place was Judenfrei, "free of Jews."
Surely you can protect your staff. Science shouldn't be a tool of politics.
But what can I do? It is the law.
But how can something so lawless be a law?
Planck's solution was to arrange a meeting with Hitler.
It is an honor.
He began by assuring Hitler that he could rely on the KWI's complete support.
Planck stressed the importance of the research they did, how it would help the Fatherland. Hitler agreed. The Reich needed clever scientists, the right kind. Not Jews.
Maybe *some* Jews. Fritz Haber may be Jewish, but he's a patriotic German. His work made a critical difference in the Great War. Don't sweep out the good with the bad.
There are no good Jews! They clump together like burrs. Where you find one, you find others.
But there's a difference between those who are deeply German.
NO!
I don't object to Jews—I object to communists. And all Jews are communists.
There is no Jewish worthiness.
Planck's apology only upset Hitler more.
People say I suffer from nervous weakness.
THIS IS SLANDER! I HAVE NERVES OF STEEL!
Planck didn't dare say another word. He backed out of the room.

Whole books have been written about Planck's struggle to keep his principles intact during the Third Reich. He kept Jewish scientists employed for as long as he could. He helped them find positions in other countries. And in 1938, when the Nazis took over the Prussian Academy of Sciences, he resigned as president in protest. Planck continued to champion Einstein and the theories of quantum physics. But he didn't actively protest. He didn't leave the country, and he continued to do research under the Reich.

Planck didn't like the Nazis' methods, but he still hoped that something good would come from the renewed patriotism and national spirit. Hahn agreed, going so far as to defend Hitler as someone who "lived almost like a saint." Planck was so sure that the Nazi tactics were temporary, he advised a Jewish colleague: "Take a pleasant trip abroad . . . And when you return all the unpleasant features of our present government will have disappeared."

Szilard, the physicist who had left rather than continue to teach with Meitner until he would be fired, described this strange acceptance from his colleagues: "They all thought that civilized Germans would not stand for anything really rough happening . . . They asked, 'Well, suppose I would oppose this thinking, what good would I do? . . . I would just lose my influence. Then why should I oppose it?' You see, the moral point of view was completely absent or very weak."

This was the argument with Planck that Meitner couldn't win. With his capitulation to the anti-Jewish laws, she saw her beloved adopted country disappearing. Germany was now a fascist dictatorship, intent on ridding itself of all Jews.

And still Meitner stayed.

FIFTEEN

TO GO OR TO STAY

Meitner found herself more and more isolated. Scientists who had been friendly now ignored her. All the German Jews had left, but as an Austrian Jew, she still had her lab.

Instead of worrying about herself, she fretted about her nephew Otto Robert Frisch, a young physicist. He had lost his place working with Otto Stern in Hamburg when Stern, also Jewish, fled to America.

Don't worry, Auntie Lise. I'll find something.

In fact, Frisch had landed a fellowship to work with Enrico Fermi in Rome. Fermi was doing work similar to Hahn's and Meitner's and getting a lot of attention for it.

But when Frisch was kicked out of Hamburg, he lost his eligibility for the fellowship (being no longer a "professional"). He couldn't go to Rome, and now no institution in Germany or Austria would accept a Jew.

Frisch left for London and found a job at a small college. It wasn't prestigious. It didn't pay well. But it was something. Frisch urged his aunt to do the same. But as she had so many times before, Meitner refused.

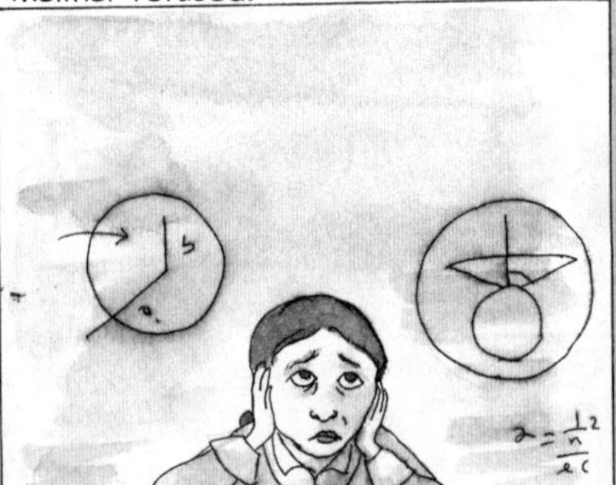

American and British universities were crowded with talented, big-name Jewish scientists. Why would they want a woman? She didn't feel welcome.

Within the four walls of her lab, she felt safe. For now.

In Berlin, the changes came quickly, one after another. Soon after German Jews were thrown out of their workplaces, Meitner was asked to register officially as a "non-Aryan." Science was especially targeted to be "cleansed of Jews." Though only 1 percent of the population, Jews represented 20 percent of the scientists in Germany. As Philipp Lenard, the ardent Nazi and Nobel laureate, wrote: "With the massive introduction of Jews into influential positions also at universities and academies, the basis of all scientific knowledge, the observation of nature itself, was forgotten and was no longer considered valid . . . The most prominent example of the damaging influence by Jews on science is provided by Mr. Einstein with his 'theories.'" Of all the sciences, Meitner's beloved physics was the one that had become a special Nazi target.

Hahn, safely Aryan himself, returned to Berlin from his semester in America in July 1933. Though he'd complained about the news media exaggerating the treatment of Jews in Germany, when he saw how many friends and colleagues had disappeared from the University of Berlin, he resigned in protest and suggested that Planck mobilize senior scientists to speak up for their Jewish colleagues. Planck refused, saying that would only make the situation worse. If he managed to find 30 men to speak out, another 150 would protest against them, eager to take over the positions suddenly left open. There would never be enough scientists willing to take the risk. Instead, they would be greatly outnumbered by those eager to push "Aryan" science and their own careers. Planck wasn't being cynical, just realistic.

From the United States, Einstein wrote to friends in Germany, asking for help with his property as the Reich seized all his assets—his bank accounts, his apartment, his summer home. There was nothing left for him to go home to, and with Hitler in power, Einstein stayed in America. The whole international physics community knew about the harassment he faced. There were quiet murmurs of support but no angry speeches, no public demonstrations. The broader public had so little interest in what happened to Jews throughout the world that newspapers didn't even mention the changes.

In Germany, the streets were filled with marching soldiers. Nazi flags and banners hung from every public building, including the institute and university. A choking militarism rippled through cities and villages as loudspeakers blared speeches and squadrons marched in shiny black boots. Hitler was keeping his promise, returning Germany to its former greatness. Food was still scarce, but a new nationalism fed the public with a satisfying pride. If the people couldn't have full bellies, at least they had a new confidence. So long as they weren't Jewish.

SIXTEEN

THE NAZIFICATION OF SCIENCE

September 6, 1933: Meitner heard the news she'd been dreading. Rust, the Prussian minister of education, removed her from the University of Berlin. She could no longer teach.

Meitner had obediently filled out the form in April, and here was the result. It hadn't occurred to her to lie about being non-Aryan.

Meitner asked Planck to intercede for her, to explain the value of her work. Planck had already tried once for Haber. He wouldn't for Meitner. A woman was a much weaker case.

FRAU MEITNER:
HEIL HITLER!

Hahn, though, wrote to Rust, explaining Meitner's importance. The answer was silence, and Hahn pushed no further.

That same month, Planck asked Hahn to act as provisional head of the KWI for Chemistry, replacing Haber. Hahn took the position.

Hahn did what Haber had refused to do, firing almost everyone at the KWI for Chemistry to allow the arriving Nazi-appointed director a clean slate.

All employees would now be members of the Nazi party, and research would be focused on poison gases. Hahn insisted he'd only done what he'd been forced to do, calling it an "unpleasant, thankless task." With Meitner, he walked a tightrope, advocating for her position but never so strongly as to jeopardize his own. The association with her was already hurting him. "The presence of . . . L. Meitner did not make the situation better. Thus at the yearly meetings of the KWI, I was always seated in a less prestigious place at the dinner table than was appropriate for my position and my age and my length of service." He described these insults as "painful experiences." When it was clear that working with a Jew would seriously damage his reputation, Hahn ended their partnership. He still turned to her constantly to interpret results in terms of physics, since he could understand them only in terms of chemistry, but the days of submitting papers together were over. Meitner's name was stripped from those they'd previously published, part of the Jewish purge from academia.

Meitner found herself being erased. Nobody could take

away the prizes she'd already won, but she was no longer the little woman with the big brain. She was "the Jewess," whispered about in the hallways as a political liability. Kurt Hess, an avid Nazi who now headed the KWI for Chemistry, argued for expulsion, insisting that "the Jewess endangers the institute." Although Meitner could no longer teach, she still had her lab. She couldn't join the Wednesday meetings, couldn't speak in public about her research, had no official status at all, but at least she could do her work. Alone, with no students, assistants, or colleagues, just her and physics. In her middle age, she was going back to her early days of scrimping and working, with no salary and no title, back to another kind of basement.

Hahn needed a new partner, but not finding a physicist to join him, he turned to Fritz Strassmann, a younger analytical chemist. Strassmann admired Meitner and was dismayed that he was replacing her simply because she was Jewish. Unlike Hahn, Strassmann took an active stand against the Nazis. In 1933, Strassmann resigned from the German Chemical Society to protest the Nazi takeover of the organization. He was blacklisted and out of work until Hahn, with Meitner's urging, got him a low-paying position as an assistant. As Hahn's partner, he could have made more money, except he refused to join the

Nazi party; as punishment, his pay was cut to one-fourth of what it should have been. Meitner, aware that Strassmann was supporting a young family, suggested that Hahn pay Strassmann extra money out of the chemistry department's private contingency fund.

When staff or colleagues had problems, they never went to Hahn for help. They turned to Meitner, even after she lost her official title. She would then talk to Hahn or Planck or Laue. As one of the staff wrote, "She was the true life and soul of the institute." Meitner cared deeply for all of her colleagues. Her vacations had been outings with fellow physicists. They were her family.

So naturally Meitner supported Strassmann. She didn't see him as taking her rightful place but as much-needed help for Hahn. She respected the young chemist's thorough work. And she was grateful for his anti-Nazi stance. She didn't know it went beyond passive resistance. When a biology professor at the University of Berlin asked for Strassmann's help hiding Andrea Wolffenstein, a Jewish woman fleeing the Gestapo (the Nazi secret police), he didn't hesitate. He immediately took a complete stranger into his apartment. He risked not only his own life but those of his wife and three-year-old son. His downstairs neighbors were vocal Nazis, so Strassmann knew he couldn't safely shelter Wolffenstein for long, but he kept her until a safer place could be found.

Fritz Haber had left Germany for a position at the University of Cambridge in England (which seems to have forgiven him for his work on chemical weapons used against British soldiers). But before he could do any new research, he died of a heart attack on January 29, 1934. Planck, who had fought so hard to keep Haber at the KWI, waited to see what the official commemoration would be. After all, Haber was a war hero who had not only produced "bread from air" (his process to create fertilizer chemically) but also made "gunpowder from air" (with his other use of ammonia synthesis). The Great War would have been lost even sooner without his inventions. But all of that was tarnished by his being Jewish, despite his Lutheran conversion. Meitner realized her own baptism was no protection at all.

Month after month passed with no official word about a send-off for such an important scientist. There wasn't even an obituary. Laue ended up bravely writing one for a newspaper and was hounded as a "Jew lover." Only the "von" in his name (Max von Laue) saved him from worse troubles. Sounding aristocratic, he was left alone.

Planck decided that he would organize a memorial ceremony himself. He scheduled it for a year after Haber's death, on January 29, 1935, and sent out invitations to the members of the German Physical and Chemical Societies in Berlin, to university faculty, to researchers at the KWI, and to the chemical industry. On January 17, 1935, the Berlin newspaper reported the upcoming ceremony. In response to the subversive announcement, Rust, the minister of education, sent out a warning that under no circumstances would anyone working for the state (meaning university professors) be permitted to attend such a gathering.

Meitner was worried that Planck was making himself into a target—or worse, that she would become one. She was torn between wanting to honor someone she very much admired and wanting to avoid more problems with the Nazis. Haber, after all, was dead, beyond caring whether there was any kind of commemoration. His family no longer lived in Germany and wouldn't be there to see him honored. Still, Planck insisted that threats wouldn't keep him away: "I will perform the ceremony, unless I am taken away by the police." He may not have been able to convince Hitler to spare such an eminent scientist in life, but this was one small thing he could do after Haber's death.

Hahn described Planck as "excited and pleased that the

ceremony will take place in spite of all the odds, unless perhaps . . . a group sent by the [Nazi] party will try to prevent us from entering by force."

At the entrance to the hall, a notice board warned in large letters:

All members of [KWI], all university faculty members, all members of groups in the Reich Association of Technical-Scientific Work . . . [are] forbidden to take part in the memorial ceremony for the Jew Fritz Haber.

Hahn and Planck opened the door and walked in. Meitner followed, trying to calm her jittery nerves.

The auditorium was packed.

As Hahn wrote, "The lovely large reception hall of Harnack House . . . was full . . . Most of those present were women, the wives of Berlin professors [or] of members of the Kaiser Wilhelm Society . . . They came as representatives of their husbands who had been prevented by a brutal prohibition from bidding their final farewell to an important person and scientist.

"Privy councilor Planck gave the introductory address, pointing out that had Haber not made his magnificent [ammonia synthesis] discovery, Germany would have collapsed, economically and militarily, in the first three months of World War I."

Despite the warnings not to attend, an eager crowd listened, including representatives from IG Farben. The Nazi government may have detested Haber as a Jew, but the German chemical industry valued him highly for his contributions in producing both fertilizer to nourish crops and toxic gases to kill enemies–a strangely mixed legacy. Nazi soldiers stood at the back of the hall, filling the room with tension, but the speeches went on as planned, music was played, and then it was over. The soldiers opened the doors and formed a line on either side of the exit, waiting for the businessmen from IG Farben to file out. Even the Nazis wanted support from the big chemical corporations. Planck strode out, head held high. Meitner held her breath as she left the hall, expecting to be pulled aside at any second. But the soldiers stood quietly. Nobody was arrested. Not even the Jews in the audience.

SEVENTEEN

CAN IT GET WORSE?

Toward the end of that year, in September 1935, the Nuremberg Laws were passed.

The Law for the Protection of German Blood and Honor

All relationships between Jews and Germans are illegal. The purity of German heritage must be protected from "the stain of the Jewish people."

The Law of Citizenship

Only people of "German-related blood" can be citizens. No Jews, who are "enemies of the race-based State."

(This law was later expanded to also exclude Black and Romani-Gypsy people.)

Civil Society Laws

Jews cannot do business with non-Jews.

Jews cannot travel.

Jews cannot ride on a bus or tram.

Jews cannot leave the country unless they surrender 90 percent of all assets to the State.

Jews cannot go to school.

Again, international scientists hesitated to speak up in support of their Jewish German colleagues. There were no protests, no public outrage.

Meitner felt completely isolated. People she had admired and trusted, people she thought admired and trusted her, stayed silent in the face of this hatred.

Two thousand scientists who were either Jewish or married to Jews fled Germany. And they turned out to be the lucky ones.

Meitner heard terrible stories, like what happened to Max Born, a fellow proponent of quantum physics. Born left Germany in 1934 for Britain. Heisenberg came to see him there with an official offer from the Nazi government: Born would not be allowed to teach in Göttingen, but he could continue to do his important research, despite being a Jew. It was a generous proposal, Heisenberg insisted. Born was tempted, but when it was clear his family couldn't join him, he refused. When Born and his wife went back to Göttingen to pack up some of the possessions the family had left behind in their rush to leave, it became clear they would never be able to return to Germany. One of his colleagues described what happened:

"H[eisenberg] was by then a professor at Göttingen, and when the Borns went to visit him, they were met with anti-Jewish sneers and obscenities, and in the end, H[eisenberg] spat on the floor at Max Born's feet! . . . Later Mrs. Born gave me her version and ended with a statement that I have never forgotten. She said simply at the end, 'And my poor Max wept.'"

Meitner knew Heisenberg personally and was disgusted by his actions. She wouldn't have thought him so cruel. She wondered which of her friends and colleagues she could really trust when it mattered most.

EIGHTEEN

THE NEW RADIOACTIVE PHYSICS

Meitner's specialty, radioactive physics, was developing in fascinating ways. She poured her attention into science, trying to ignore what was happening politically and socially. And there was a lot to focus on.

Fermi in Rome was bombarding elements with neutrons and getting interesting results. The neutrons hit the nucleus and supposedly released new isotopes, heavier than the original element. These new elements were called "transuranics" —elements heavier than uranium, the heaviest known natural element. Everyone rushed to copy Fermi and find more transuranics.

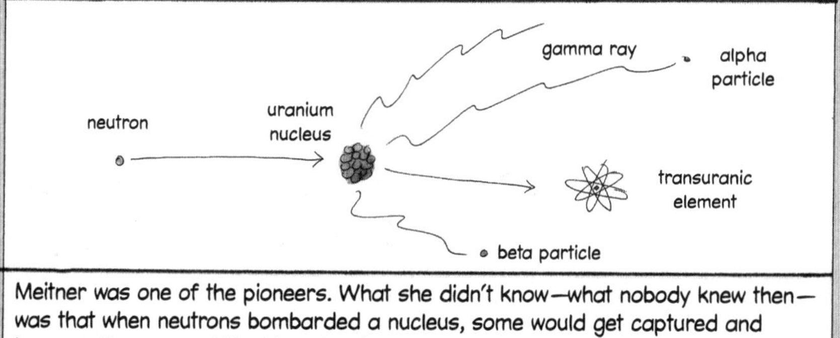
gamma ray
alpha particle
neutron
uranium nucleus
transuranic element
beta particle

Meitner was one of the pioneers. What she didn't know—what nobody knew then—was that when neutrons bombarded a nucleus, some would get captured and increase the mass of the atom, turning the uranium into a heavier isotope. To think that an atom would get bigger rather than smaller when hit with neutrons was counterintuitive. And something else entirely was also happening. Meitner's discovery of it would make all this early work a mere footnote in the history of physics.

After not working with her for years, Hahn and his new partner, Strassmann, started collaborating with Meitner on this new avenue. They talked about the experiments they would set up, what they were looking for, and how to understand the results, something Hahn couldn't do without her. He needed her enough to risk having his name alongside hers. Radioactive elements were a subject for chemists, as Marie Curie had shown, but neutron bombardment on uranium moved the question into the realm of physics, necessitating an understanding of atomic structure. The team published eight articles on transuranics in 1935 and 1936 (with Meitner, like so many years before, listed now as L. Meitner to avoid once again the bias against women scientists). They were an essential part of the conversation among scientists trying to figure out what transuranics were and how they were created on an atomic level.

The results turned out to be hard to interpret—so messy and complicated, in fact, that Fermi stopped working on transuranics completely, worried about the contradictory data he was getting.

Hahn, Strassmann, and Meitner continued their transuranic research. In the fall of 1936, Hahn was invited to lecture on his work to the German Chemical Society. Despite the dangers of being associated with a Jew, Hahn took a daring stand. He declined the invitation since Meitner, his partner in this research, wasn't also invited. He wrote to a friend, explaining that "one hears only my name for investigations which Lise Meitner engaged in as fully as I. The reason for this is, of course, related to [political] conditions we can do nothing about. But I think it is not quite right when I take credit for overall intellectual property that is not mine exclusively." It was a rare recognition of Meitner's important role in their work together—something Hahn wouldn't repeat when it mattered much more.

NINETEEN

THE JEWESS MUST GO

For a while, Meitner felt safe. After all, she wasn't a German Jew. She was Austrian. Her parents and siblings were fine in Vienna.

She couldn't teach, but she could still do research and live in her KWI-owned apartment. She was all too aware of the anti-Jewish laws but didn't imagine she would be arrested.

Meitner wanted to continue her work in Berlin, but concerned scientists from all over the world were trying to find her a job outside Germany. Sweden, the Netherlands, Denmark, Britain, and the United States were all explored, but with so many Jewish refugees, there were no offers. And without a lab to go to, Meitner wouldn't leave.

If she couldn't do physics, what was the point?

JEWS NOT WANTED HERE!
SS

March 1938: Germany invaded Austria.

Suddenly, Meitner's Austrian passport was worthless. Now she couldn't get out of Germany, and she couldn't get into any other country. She had no legal status at all.

As Meitner's position became more precarious, the rhetoric against Jewish scientists got uglier. In April 1938, Johannes Stark, the renowned physicist who promoted "Aryan physics," wrote an article titled "The 'Jewish Spirit' in Science" for the journal *Nature*:

> In July of last year, several correspondents sent us copies of an article entitled . . . 'White Jews in Science' . . . The main theme was that it was not sufficient to exclude all Jews from sharing in the political, cultural and economic life of the nation, but to exterminate the Jewish spirit, which is stated to be the most clearly recognizable in the field of physics, and its most significant representative Professor Einstein . . . To purge science from this Jewish spirit is our most urgent task. For science represents the key position from which intellectual Judaism can always regain a significant influence on all spheres of national life . . .

Meitner was closely associated with a brand of science that the Reich wanted to "exterminate." The new head of the Kaiser Wilhelm Institute for Chemistry, the Nazi Kurt Hess, wanted her gone.

Meitner could no longer hide in her lab. Choices she thought she would always have no longer existed. Nervously, Meitner asked Hahn to speak up for her, to let Hess know how important her work was. This time, Hahn refused. He couldn't respond to Meitner's fears. He had his own–Meitner was causing trouble for the KWI. With her there, they risked losing government money and support. Instead of defending his partner and colleague, he pressured Meitner to resign. She was the only Jewish person left, and nobody wanted her there. Meitner felt trapped, scared, and sad. She wrote in her diary: "Hahn says I should not come to the Institute anymore."

She went to the lab anyway. Hahn told her to leave. It was a deep and lasting betrayal. She added to the pages she'd been writing, "He has in essence thrown me out." Hahn wrote his own notes: "Lise was very unhappy and angry with me now I too had left her in the lurch."

Only a few colleagues defended her. One was Carl Bosch, the head of the Kaiser Wilhelm Society after Planck retired. When Hahn went to him, suggesting they push Meitner to resign as a solution to their "distracting Jewish problem," Bosch snapped that the society was under his direction, not the government's, and Meitner should stay.

The next thing Meitner was told was to give up was her apartment. It was official KWI housing, after all. She couldn't expect to stay now that she no longer held a position. Other scientists were already in line, waiting to live in her home of many decades. Deeply depressed, Meitner moved to a room at the Hotel Adlon. Not knowing what else to do, Meitner continued to go to the lab despite Hahn's refusal to work with her anymore. She clung to every scrap of normal life she could find, living off her meager savings.

Meitner didn't know she was on a list of undesirables. A scientific newspaper would later report: "In almost no other science did Nordic men in Germany take a more active part than in physics. But also none has the same sorry distinction of producing a Jew like Einstein . . . The Jewish-minded influence of the councillors of the former Kaiser Wilhelm II was devastating, and their confidence was repaid by the Jewry world-wide in true Jewish style. The founding of the Kaiser Wilhelm Institutes in Dahlem was the prelude to a flood of Jews into physical science. The Jew Haber . . . *the Jewess Lise Meitner* (my italics), James Franck . . . Niels David Bohr." A long list of Jews and the descriptions of where they now worked followed, showing that most of the Jewish taint had been cleared out. Meitner was the only one still at the institute. The others, all men, had fled for positions in Britain and the United States.

While nobody in Germany offered help, colleagues abroad reached out. A Swiss physicist invited her to give a lecture in Zurich. James Franck thought he could get her something at the University of Chicago, and Niels Bohr invited her to his institute in Copenhagen. Bohr's offer was the most inviting and concrete. It meant an actual position at an excellent lab. Thrown out of her home and her work, completely alone, Meitner was finally ready to leave Berlin. She told Bohr she would come to Copenhagen.

But Denmark wasn't willing to take her. How could the Danish consulate give her a visa when her Austrian passport was no longer valid?

Bosch, furious that Hahn had gotten his way, did what he could to help Meitner. He tried to get her a state exit permit that would allow "travel" abroad (travel meaning leaving Germany for good). He wrote to Wilhelm Frick, the Reich minister of the interior, asking for Meitner to receive official permission to go to a neutral country–Sweden, Denmark, or Switzerland.

"Miss Meitner," Bosch explained, "is non-Aryan; nonetheless, with the concurrence of all the official departments, she has been allowed to retain her position as she is engaged in important scientific discoveries . . . I find it very desirable if it would be made possible to come to a smooth resolution of this case . . . It is only a question of obtaining for Miss Meitner, who has an Austrian passport, notice that she may return to Germany—otherwise, travel abroad for purposes of employment is impossible—or that Miss Meitner be issued a German passport. Heil Hitler!"

The tortured way this letter is written shows how desperately Bosch wanted to convince Nazi authorities of the "desirable" outcome he hoped for. First, he presented Miss Meitner, though non-Aryan, as a good non-Aryan. Then he offered two different solutions to the problem—an exit visa assuring the country she went to that Miss Meitner intended to return to Germany, that her travel was temporary and for work purposes only. Or simply the issuance of a valid German passport that would allow her to apply for a visa abroad. The letter ended as all official correspondence did, pledging loyalty to Hitler.

The answer came a couple of weeks later. Bosch called Meitner at her hotel, and she wrote down what he read to her:

> By order of the Reichminister Dr. Fr[ick], may I most respectfully inform you in answer to your

> letter of the 20th last month that there are political objections to the issuing of an Ausland pass [an exit visa or passport for travel abroad] to Prof. M[eitner]. It is considered undesirable that renowned Jews should leave Germany for abroad to act there against the interests of Germany according to their inner persuasion as representatives of the German sciences.

Meitner couldn't earn money. She couldn't do physics. And now she couldn't leave Germany. She was trapped.

TWENTY
PASSPORT PROBLEMS

Meitner felt forgotten, but she wasn't. A community of scientists tried to figure how to get her safely out of Germany.
Paul Scherrer, the Swiss physicist who had invited Meitner to Zurich, thought a forged passport could work.
Paul Rosbaud, the science editor who had published many of Meitner's papers, might have been able to get a fake passport. He had sent his Jewish wife and daughter to safety in England but stayed in Germany to sabotage the Nazis. He worked with British intelligence and wanted Meitner as a source for information.
Niels Bohr wrote to colleagues, searching for a way to get her into Denmark without papers.
Adriaan Fokker, a Dutch physicist, worried that Meitner would be caught if she tried to leave. He feared she'd be sent to a prison camp. He wanted to ask Hahn for help but didn't trust him.
Dirk Coster, another Dutch physicist, thought Meitner had to risk leaving. Things were getting even worse for the Jews, labeled "undesirables" with no legal rights.
The idea of a forged passport shocked Meitner. She tried to find her own way to leave.
Diary entry, June 15, 1938: "Went for information. Hear that technical and academic [people] will not be permitted to get out."
No position was found, but that didn't matter anymore. Coster and Fokker decided that Meitner had to escape. There was no other choice.

Once the decision was made to get Meitner out of the Reich, the question was how. The scientists wanted to present her with a path forward in physics so that Meitner would take the risk to flee. Fokker and Coster asked the Dutch Ministry of Education to allow Meitner into the Netherlands, though she had no passport. The ministry warned that without a formal offer of a position at a university or research institute, Meitner could not get an entry visa. Also, the ministry reminded the scientists, foreigners were not allowed to work for pay. Meitner would have to get a lecturer position, something that entailed faculty approval. It was summer, classes were out, and professors were hard to reach. It wasn't likely that Meitner would get the offer she needed for this kind of entry visa.

Fokker and Coster didn't give up. They turned next to the Dutch Ministry of Justice. They also reached out to get funding for Meitner, writing to people like the heads of the X-ray division of Philips NV and other radiation industries in the Netherlands. They collected small contributions, but nothing substantial. If Meitner couldn't work for a salary, what would she live on? Already sixty years old, would she be able to collect her pension from the KWI? Knowing how the Nazis seized Jewish assets, it seemed unlikely. But money was the least of their problems. How would Meitner get across the border safely?

It was late in June 1938, and Coster feared waiting any longer. By the time the Ministry of Justice answered them, Meitner could be in a prison camp.

Meanwhile, in Copenhagen, Bohr was also trying to find a position for Meitner. He knew she was more likely to take the risk of crossing the border illegally if she had a lab waiting for her. She was a scientist any country should eagerly welcome, having by then been nominated for the Nobel Prize nineteen times. Sweden, as a neutral country, seemed especially promising. Manne Siegbahn, a physicist colleague, was building a new research institute for physics in Stockholm. Although he was focused on the big machinery of a new cyclotron, a particle accelerator that would allow a closer view of atomic behavior, he agreed to find a place for Meitner. Her kind of experimental work didn't demand much space or expensive equipment.

Not trusting the mail, Siegbahn sent a professor to Berlin to talk to Meitner directly. The messenger found Meitner in her hotel and offered her a one-year salaried position at the new Stockholm institute. Meitner wasn't sure what to do—she still hoped she could work with Bohr at his institute. And she had already accepted that position. Could she agree to another one? After all, she had no papers to get into either Sweden or Denmark. Besides, working with Bohr would be an exciting challenge. She wasn't so sure about Siegbahn. She knew it was ridiculous to be picky at such a time, but she couldn't help herself. Having the right place to do her work mattered more to her than food, comfort, even safety. The professor assured her this offer came through Bohr, that he had convinced Siegbahn to open his doors to her. There would be time later for Meitner to go to Copenhagen. The important thing now was to get out of Germany and into a country that would accept her.

Peter Debye, the Dutch physicist who had taken over as head of the KWI's physics department after Einstein left, followed the orders to rid his section of "non-Aryan elements" but didn't force Jews to resign until December 1938. That summer, he still hoped Meitner could stay. But when Coster told him of the plan to get Meitner out of Germany and into the Netherlands, Debye agreed it was for the best. He told her about the money Coster had collected to support her, at least for a while. She would be safe in the Netherlands, but there would be no access to a lab. Meitner now had at least some kind of choice—Sweden or the Netherlands. Physics mattered more than anything else, so Meitner told Debye she would go to Sweden after all.

Debye wrote this news in a coded message to Coster, regretting that Meitner wouldn't go to the Netherlands as Coster hoped. But she would be working, contributing to the growing understanding of radioactive elements and atomic structure.

It all seemed settled. Meitner would leave her home city of the past thirty years. She would go to a new country, with a new language. The move from Vienna to Berlin had been easy—everyone spoke German. Meitner worried about learning Swedish. How would she do it, old as she was? She wouldn't be able to take any of her equipment, few of her books. Just some clothes, a toothbrush, the most basic things.

As Meitner worried about leaving her lab, news came from Bohr: The visa and position in Sweden were not yet "in order." The clock was ticking. Each day in Germany seemed full of danger. The borders were still relatively open for those with the right papers, but the political speeches on the radio grew more and more heated, blaming Jews for all of Germany's problems. The sense of impending doom hung heavy in the city, marked by the drumming feet of Nazi storm troopers and soldiers. Signs forbidding Jews entry hung in most shop windows. The order for Jews to wear the yellow star, marking them as noncitizens with no rights, wouldn't happen until 1941, but there was a growing sense that more punishing measures were coming.

On July 4, 1938, Bosch warned Hahn that Meitner was in danger. He had heard that the new policy prohibiting scientists from leaving Germany would be strictly enforced. Meitner would never get permission to leave. The only way for her to get out was illegally. Risky, yes, but staying was even more dangerous. What did Hahn do with this information? He didn't want to get in trouble with the authorities, so he didn't mention it to Meitner. Instead, he told Peter Debye.

Debye went right to Meitner. The Nazis could easily decide to arrest all Jewish scientists to keep them from fleeing. It didn't matter what kind of position or salary was offered; the crucial thing was for Meitner to leave as soon as possible. Meitner, so stubborn about leaving before, realized she had no choice. Long ago, her father had told her how courageous she was, fighting for her place in the world of physics, but all she felt now was dread.

Debye wrote to Coster in the coded language they had agreed on:

"The assistant we talked about, who had made what seemed like a firm decision, sought me out once again . . . He is now completely convinced (this happened in the last few days) that he would rather go to Groningen, indeed that this is the only avenue open to him . . . if you were to come rather soon, as if you received an SOS, that would give my wife and me even greater pleasure."

The male assistant was code for Meitner. Groningen was the university town in the Netherlands where Coster worked. Debye cloaked the urgency of his invitation by phrasing it as a friendly visit with colleagues. Coster should come stay with Debye's family and take the assistant back to work with him in Groningen. What could be more innocent? What could attract the censor's eye?

The letter, sent by regular mail, took several days to reach Coster. He had to act immediately–no more waiting for the post! His answer was a telegram to Debye:

SAT 9 JULY/ I AM COMING TO
LOOK OVER THE ASSISTANT; IF HE SUITS ME
I WILL TAKE HIM BACK WTH ME.

Help, Coster wanted Meitner to know, was on the way.

TWENTY-ONE

HOW TO SMUGGLE A SCIENTIST

How to get Meitner safely across the border? Coster told Fokker that the plan was back on—they had to get Meitner to the Netherlands. Fokker called the Ministry of Justice to check on the status of the application they had already submitted for her, but it was Saturday. They had to wait until Monday.

Instead, Fokker called the office of the Dutch Border Guards and managed to reach the director. He explained that Meitner was an important scientist who needed to get into the Netherlands without papers. The director was sympathetic and said he'd have an answer on Monday.

Meanwhile, Coster packed a bag, bought a train ticket for Berlin, and started pacing the floor, waiting for the go-ahead from Fokker.

Meitner knew nothing of all this. She was still waiting for Bohr to tell her that Sweden was okay.

On Monday morning, the Dutch Ministry of Justice told Fokker that Meitner had provisional entry into the Netherlands. Written confirmation would follow. Fokker gave Coster the news. He didn't wait for any letter but rushed to the station. The word of the ministry would have to be enough. Fokker would let the Dutch Border Guards know.

In Berlin, Debye was anxiously waiting for Coster. He sent a telegram to Fokker.

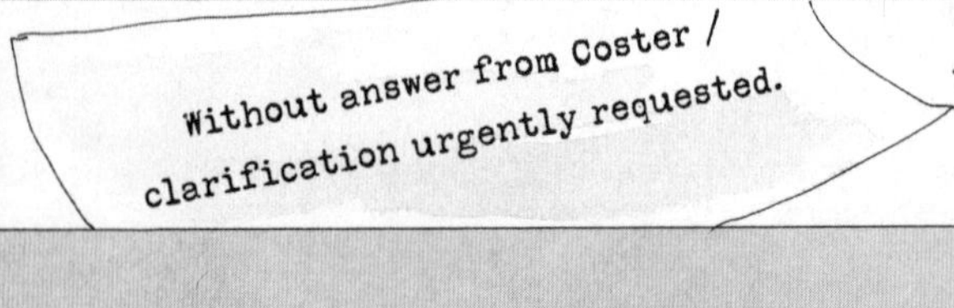
Without answer from Coster /
clarification urgently requested.

Fokker sent a telegram reply: Coster on his way. The plan was set into motion.

On board the Groningen-Berlin train, a trip he had taken many times before, Coster was acutely aware of the Nazi soldiers everywhere. At the border, they strode up and down the aisles, checking and rechecking passports. People whose papers weren't in order were thrown off the train or arrested. Coster looked nervously out the window, trying to look innocent. The Dutch scenery, which had been peaceful, with streams, fields, and towns of charming brick buildings, was replaced with the German militaristic landscape. Medieval buildings were cloaked in enormous banners with swastikas, their antique charm choked by the bold design. The Nazi insignia was everywhere, a reminder of the presence of Nazi eyes watching everyone and everything.

Nervously, Coster checked the documents he had brought for Meitner, hoping they were enough. He had no official passport, no visa, no entry permit. The plan was to take a small local train from Berlin to the border village of Nieuweschans in the Netherlands. Soldiers didn't bother searching that route as often, and if anything went wrong, the mayor of Nieuweschans, a good friend of Coster's, could help them. Fokker's words to the director of the Dutch Border Guards should help, too. He would show him the note of the Ministry of Justice's provisional approval (the least official document possible!) and ask that they let Coster pass with his traveling companion, no questions asked. That is, if the Nazis allowed them to leave Germany first.

That night, Coster arrived at the Berlin station late, exhausted by the tension of the last few days. Debye was waiting for him, just as anxious. Back at Debye's home, the men tried to relax, but they knew the real risks hadn't even begun yet.

Meitner, equally edgy, still hoped for news from Bohr, from Siegbahn. On Tuesday morning, she followed her usual habit of an early breakfast, then went to the KWI.

Debye hadn't been sure he could trust Hahn, but now that the time had come, he decided to give him a chance. Meitner would want to say goodbye. Debye told Hahn about Coster's plan, and together they explained to Meitner that she wouldn't be going to Sweden but to the Netherlands. All the arrangements and approvals had been taken care of, they assured her. The only thing was, she had to leave early the next morning. No more hesitating.

Hahn offered to help Meitner pack and suggested she spend her last night at his home. He told people at the KWI she would be away visiting family and even marked his calendar "Meitner goes to Vienna." Nobody must think she was emigrating. He would send her things to her later. She had to look like someone taking a short trip, not a refugee fleeing the country with all of her belongings. Not that she had much anyway. It was her lab equipment that really mattered.

That last day in Berlin, Meitner kept to her regular schedule, staying at the KWI until eight p.m., keeping her mind busy proofreading an article by a young colleague. Hahn left with her, and the two went to her room to quickly pack. As instructed, Meitner didn't check out of her hotel, and the two left to spend a final evening together at Hahn's house. Meitner's neighbor at the hotel, Kurt Hess, the Nazi scientist now in charge of the KWI, watched Meitner and Hahn leave with her small bags. He was immediately suspicious. Yes, Hahn had said Meitner would be seeing her family in Austria, but Hess didn't believe it. He reported Meitner to the police as a Jewish scientist planning to sneak out of the country.

Hahn was relieved that Meitner was going, removing the Jewish stigma from the KWI, but he was scared of the very real risk he was taking by helping her even in a small way. He was also losing an important work partner, someone he couldn't replace. They would stay in touch with letters, maybe even meet in some neutral country. It was all for the best. Meitner tried to see it that way, too, but she felt exiled from everything that mattered most to her. She had spent a lifetime working hard to be taken seriously, to earn a place in the world of physics. Now all of that was lost.

The next morning, Wednesday, July 13, Rosbaud, Meitner's science editor friend, picked her up at Hahn's to take her to the train station. The time had come to say goodbye to Hahn. Meitner had relied on him to help her make her way as a woman in the male world of science. For thirty years, they had made exciting discoveries together, publishing important articles on radioactivity. Hahn's name may have always come first, but at least Meitner's was there, too. She had been hurt by his pushing her out of the KWI, but he did care, and at the last minute, he thrust something into her hand. It was small, hard, cold–his mother's ring. Meitner was confused. Why would he give her this heirloom? Hahn blushed and explained awkwardly that it wasn't a sentimental gift. It was supposed to be useful, something she could sell or use as a bribe in "urgent emergencies." Meitner took it, clasping it tightly, deeply touched by the gift. She prayed she would never need it.

Rosbaud hurried her into the car, worried she would change her mind. Coster, he assured her, would be waiting for her at the station. She was supposed to act casually, as if they had run into each other by chance. Coster would get on the train first. Meitner should sit within sight of him, but not right by him, not until they got close to the border.

Meitner clutched Hahn's ring nervously, then thrust it deep into her purse. How could this plan possibly work? The Nazis would see she had no passport and arrest her. She would be sent to one of those horrific camps she had heard about. Meitner was short and dark, not statuesque and fair. Wouldn't the soldiers know she was Jewish just by looking at her?

As the car got closer to the station, Meitner's panic grew. She begged Rosbaud to turn back, she couldn't go through with it.

Meitner didn't know that Rosbaud was a spy. He was communicating secretly with British intelligence about Nazi movements, scientific work, weapon plans. For him, this was more than taking care of an old friend–it was a mission. In fact, Meitner was about to become part of his spy network. She was too valuable a scientist to stay in Germany. Her expertise and her contacts with atomic scientists all over the world were needed.

Rosbaud soothed Meitner. There was no reason for the

Nazis to suspect she was a famous physicist. No reason for them to think she was fleeing the country. No reason to consider her Jewish. Coster would take good care of her. A whole network of scientists was working to help her, he assured her. She had more support than she knew.

The train station was crowded with soldiers and SS troops (the paramilitary branch of the Nazi party). Meitner wanted to shrink into the floor, but then she saw Coster, and his familiar, friendly face calmed her. So many people were risking so much for her—she had to be brave. Several police officers walked by, and Meitner flinched. Were they coming for her? Passengers and the SS crowded onto the train. All the uniforms made Meitner shudder as Rosbaud helped her board. He lifted her suitcases onto the overhead rack and said goodbye, nodding to Coster as he left the train car.

Meitner sat next to the window, nervously staring out at still more soldiers, all in heavy, shiny boots, carrying heavy, shiny rifles. Every time the SS walked by, she held her breath. She clutched her purse, too nervous to read, staring anxiously out the window. Outside of Berlin, even the smallest German village was draped in Nazi banners. There was no escaping the shadow of the Reich. Had she waited too long?

TWENTY-TWO

SUCCESS OR FAILURE?

Hahn wrote in his autobiography, "With fear and trembling we wondered if she would get through or not. We agreed upon a code word by which we were to be informed by telegram on the success or failure of the journey. Lise Meitner was especially exposed to the danger of repeated controls by the SS in the trains going abroad. Time and again, people who had tried to go abroad had been arrested on trains and brought back."

After seven long hours, the train neared the border with the Netherlands. Coster moved to sit next to Meitner, as if he'd just noticed that his colleague was on the same train. He tried to be reassuring.

All will be okay.
Will it?

Coster explained that the Dutch immigration officers at Nieuweschans knew about her situation and not only would let Meitner in but also would use "friendly persuasion" with the German border guards.

But what about the SS? Friendly persuasion wouldn't work with them. And what about the police that Hess had notified about Meitner's escape?

Maybe the authorities hadn't gotten the message in time, Hess later complained to Hahn. Stern-faced police had filled the Berlin station, but none had boarded the train. In fact, Hess's complaint had been sent to a scientist at the KWI to check on its validity. Was Meitner missing? The scientist's response, unfortunately for Hess, was slow, deliberately slow.

The train stopped at the border for Dutch and German officials to look at passengers' documents. Sure enough, the Dutch border guards walked right past Coster and Meitner. But the German border guards asked for Coster's passport. Meitner thought she would faint, her mouth dry as she waited for the soldiers to demand her papers. She reached into her purse, gripping Hahn's ring tightly and steeling herself for the worst as the guards handed back Coster's papers.

Meitner sat rigidly still, every muscle tense. But the soldiers turned away and walked on. Who cared about an older woman, after all? After a lifetime of fighting for a place as a woman, feeling her skirts drag her down, those same skirts now acted as a magical cloak. Traveling with her "husband," Meitner had become invisible.

The SS and German guards got off, and the train crossed into the Netherlands. Meitner and Coster were both stunned, not quite believing what had just happened. Meitner gulped in air, daring to breathe again. It was the first time, the only time, Meitner felt lucky to be a woman, easily ignored.

Meitner, shaking, stared out the window again, only now the landscape was friendly and charming–farmers' fields, grazing cows, small towns with church spires. This was what normal life was like, Meitner thought, blinking through tears. It was what Germany had been like before it became a fascist state. You forget what it was supposed to be like, Meitner noted later in her diary.

Coster smiled. He had been struck by the difference as well, though from the other direction, going from his charming university town to oppressive Berlin.

Safely in Dutch territory, Meitner and Coster could talk freely. He told her about the money collected for her, though he was still working to get her some kind of position. Meitner hoped that a place in Sweden would work out, as Bohr had promised. She was an exile from her home, her language, her lab. She couldn't bear to be an exile from physics.

It was getting dark when the train arrived at Groningen station. Coster's car was where he had left it, just as it should be. He loaded Meitner's small suitcases, and the two drove to his home. Meitner was numb with shock, Coster jangly with nerves. But the night air smelled especially sweet. Meitner was free.

TWENTY-THREE

A NARROW ESCAPE

The next day, Coster sent the promised telegram, telling Hahn the "baby" had arrived. Hahn wired back:
I want to congratulate you/ what will be the name of your daughter?
Hahn spread the news throughout Berlin's scientific community—Meitner was safe in the Netherlands.
Did you hear?
Yes, what a relief!
Not a minute too soon!
But she still needs a lab, a position.
She has to do physics!
Fokker came to the house, eager to see that Meitner was all right. The woman he knew as shy, but smart and focused, looked hollowed out, deeply terrified. He wrote in his notes that she was in shock, "inwardly torn apart."
Coster needed to recover, too. He spent the week at home with Meitner, writing to colleagues and getting congratulatory telegrams from all over.
Wolfgang Pauli, a physicist colleague and friend of Meitner's, who had written the first review of Einstein's theory of relativity, sent Coster a telegram.
Pauli's message:
You have made yourself as famous for the abduction of Lise MEITNER as for [the discovery of] hafnium.

Safe in Groningen, Meitner heard just how narrow her escape had been. Laue wrote to her about Hess's warning to the police. Luckily, by the time the scientist had corroborated Meitner's absence, the train was safely in Dutch territory. "The shot that was to bring you down in the last minute missed you. You yourself probably did not notice it. The more so because of it, I waited for news that you had arrived safely." Meitner felt chilled all over again, thinking how close she had come to being arrested.

To friends and family, she put on a brave face, writing to them in Austria; to her nephew working in England; to Paul Scherrer, thanking him for his help getting her out of Berlin; and to Bohr, asking if there was still a chance for work in Stockholm. She deeply appreciated all that Fokker and Coster had done for her, but she needed to be independent, to earn her own way. And she needed to do physics.

She didn't have to wait long for an answer. The offer from Sweden was firm now! Meitner would take a boat to Copenhagen, stay with Bohr at his institute, then travel to Stockholm.

Meitner still had no passport, no papers, and very little

money, but Bohr had a lot of influence. He lived in the "House of Honor," a mansion given to him for lifetime use by the Carlsberg brewing company after he won the Nobel Prize in Physics in 1922. The house, besides being large and gracious, was right next door to the brewery, with beer piped in directly (another perk of the prize). A guest room was prepared for Meitner, with fresh-cut flowers and a peaceful view of the garden. Bohr's sons and their families lived with him, and the grandchildren's lively energy, the picnics on the lawn, and the intense discussions of physics were all healing for Meitner.

Meitner's physicist nephew, Otto Frisch, was also in Copenhagen, having moved to the Institute for Theoretical Physics after his time in London. So she had friends, colleagues, and family there. If only the Danish government would let her stay. But without official papers, that wasn't possible. After a month, she had to leave.

The Stockholm institute wasn't quite ready for her yet, so she took the train up the Swedish coast to Kungälv, where her old friend Eva von Bahr (by then, Bahr-Bergius) lived. Eva was a physicist, too, the first Swedish woman to become a lecturer in physics. She had taught until her supportive male colleague, Knut Ångström, died in 1910. With his death, her position disappeared, and women weren't allowed to teach again in Sweden until 1925. Just as Meitner had left Vienna for better opportunities, Eva had moved to Berlin to teach at the university. She met Meitner there and they quickly became friends.

Eva wasn't as driven as Meitner–physics wasn't her entire world. She went back to Sweden to care for her ill mother, became a high school teacher, and married a fellow teacher. Now she could provide Meitner with a lovely country escape, warm friendship, and discussions about physics, a small slice of normal life after her terrifying escape. Eva advised Meitner to retire officially from the KWI, to ask for her pension. That would take some financial pressure off Meitner, allowing her to work for free if she had to, as she'd done when she first started her career.

Meitner hated to sever all official ties with the KWI, but she had to recognize she was cut off already. With trembling hands, she wrote to Hahn, asking two enormous favors. First, could he pack up her things and ship them to her? Second, could he let the KWI know she was retiring and needed her pension?

On August 29, 1938, summer vacation was officially over and Hahn returned to the KWI with the report that Meitner had retired. The news was happily received by the administration and some of Hahn's fellow scientists, glad that the "Jewess" was gone for good. Hahn was relieved himself. He wrote an initial application for her pension, then handed over the task to Bosch. He warned Meitner that the government would be angry if they knew she had left the country.

The Ministry of Education wrote back to Hahn: "Professor Lise Meitner, previously an Austrian national, is working as a guest at the [KWI] for Chemistry. Since she has become a German national through union with Austria, it has to be established what percentage of Jewish blood she has."

This wasn't something Hahn wanted to answer. Bosch would have to respond, not Hahn.

Meanwhile, Meitner moved to Stockholm, staying in a hotel while waiting for Siegbahn's new physics institute to be finished. Construction was almost done, but the labs needed equipment and staff. Meitner would have to wait before she could get back to the transuranic research she missed so much. She wrote imploring letters to Hahn:

"Perhaps you cannot fully appreciate how unhappy it makes me to realize that you always think that I am unfair and embittered, and that you also say so to other people. If you think it over, it cannot be difficult to understand what it means to me that I have none of my scientific equipment. For me that is much harder than everything else. But I am really not embittered—it is just that I see no real purpose in my life at the moment and I am very lonely."

Meitner wrote to another friend: "I feel like a wind-up doll that automatically does certain things, gives a certain smile, and has no real life in itself." To Coster, she wrote, "One dare not look back. One cannot look forward."

To Hahn, she sent professional letters, too, guiding him to continue their experiments. She arranged to meet him that October at Bohr's lab in Copenhagen, now that she had the official papers she needed for brief visits outside Sweden. Once again, Bohr generously invited her to stay at his home. Once again, he welcomed her into the labs at his institute. Bohr was refining his model of the atom and explained his new thinking about atomic structure. He believed the atom was held together by something like the surface tension in a drop of water.

Seeing Hahn brought tears to Meitner's eyes. He was a living reminder of all that she had lost—her research, her teaching, her professional status, and her friend. He had been her friend once. She hoped he could be again.

Hahn was also moved to see Meitner. She had been an essential part of his research for most of his career. He could understand what was happening chemically when neutrons bombarded radioactive elements, but he didn't grasp what was happening in terms of physics, at the atomic level. He needed her to interpret his experiments, especially now.

Hahn showed her the results of his recent work on transuranics. He couldn't understand them and needed her to explain them to him. Hahn expected to see new, heavier isotopes as a result of the neutron bombardment, as usually happened. Instead, he was seeing lighter elements–including barium. Bohr was skeptical and wondered if Hahn had stumbled on some strange new transuranic element that he simply didn't recognize. Meitner thought it was more than that. Something was very wrong. Had Hahn been careless, allowing some kind of contamination? Meitner urged him to do the experiments all over again. Hahn thought perhaps he was finding a new kind of lighter radioactive particle instead of the transuranics everyone had been reporting. Meitner knew that wasn't what was happening. This was something else entirely, if she could only figure out what.

Hahn couldn't stay long. His wife was seriously ill. He promised to let Meitner know how the next experiments went. They may have been in different countries, and Meitner had no lab of her own to check Hahn's research, but they were working together again through the mail. Hahn ran the experiments, and Meitner interpreted the results. Just long distance, through letters. As they'd done experiments together during the Great War.

With Meitner safely far from the KWI, Hahn was fine with partnering so long as they didn't publish the results together. He couldn't be linked with a Jewish physicist. He'd made that clear to her many times before.

It wasn't the partnering Meitner wanted, but she comforted herself with the thought they were still working together in any fashion. She returned to Sweden, where the Stockholm institute was finally open and Meitner had an official place at last. There was no equipment yet, and her salary was set at the low level of an assistant who had just graduated, rather than at the high level that her experience and reputation deserved. There were many Jewish scientists in similar situations. Having fled Germany, they accepted positions much lower than those they had left behind. But no male scientist took the kind of demotion, both in pay and in status, that Meitner did. Siegbahn had felt pressured by Bohr to do something for Meitner, but he wasn't a strong supporter. She knew exactly where she stood with him—back in a basement lab, far from the important activity upstairs. She wrote, "Scientifically I am completely isolated, for months I speak with no one about physics, sit alone in my room and try to keep myself busy. You cannot call it 'work.'"

In Stockholm, that isolation was broken by the physicist Enrico Fermi and his wife, there for the 1938 Nobel Prize ceremony. They were also refugees who had fled anti-Semitism—Fermi's wife was Jewish. The three swapped stories about friends who had left Europe, hoping for safety in the United States or Britain. Fermi was heading for Columbia University in New York himself. It seemed like everyone Meitner knew was across an ocean now. She was safe but more alone than ever.

TWENTY-FOUR

A BRILLIANT ENOUGH PHYSICIST?

Even well after the start of World War II, scientists at King's College London, part of the University of London, hoped to get Meitner a position there. Better for her to work in anti-Nazi England than in neutral Sweden.

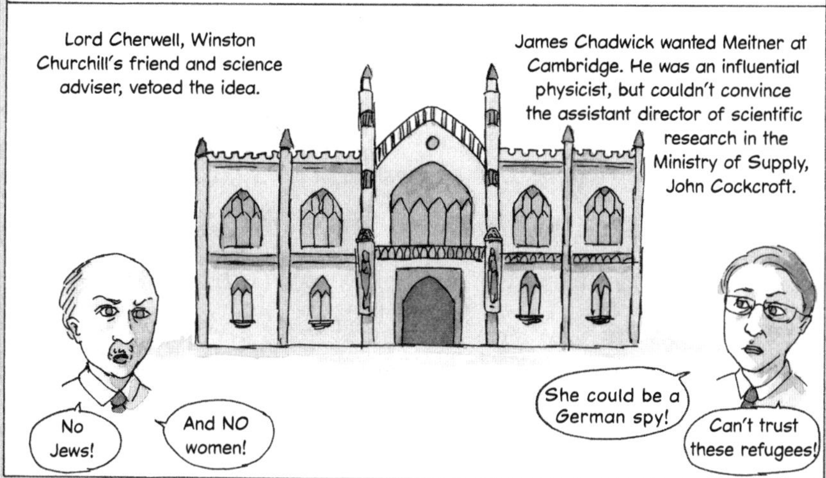
Lord Cherwell, Winston Churchill's friend and science adviser, vetoed the idea.
No Jews!
And NO women!
James Chadwick wanted Meitner at Cambridge. He was an influential physicist, but couldn't convince the assistant director of scientific research in the Ministry of Supply, John Cockcroft.
She could be a German spy!
Can't trust these refugees!

So Meitner stayed in Stockholm—which turned out to be a good place to learn about German scientific work.

Since Sweden was neutral, German scientists were allowed to travel there. Meitner talked to and wrote to everyone, and they all responded. She gave a lot of information to Rosbaud, the science editor who had helped her escape. She knew now that he used his cover as an editor to talk to scientists all over Europe, passing on important research to British intelligence. Meitner was a major source for him.

Sweden is working on producing heavy water. I'm not sure why.
How far along are they? Can you ask?
Maybe even visit the site?

October 1938 also brought word from the Ministry of Education in Berlin. Meitner's retirement was accepted and her pension granted—but the money wouldn't go to her. As a Jew, her assets had been seized.

This wasn't reassuring news. Meitner worried about her family in Austria. By then, her parents were dead and one sister had already fled to the United States, but her other brothers and sisters were still in Vienna. Meitner begged her sister Auguste to join her in Sweden. But it was too late. Justinian, Auguste's husband, had been arrested and sent to Dachau, a prison camp. Auguste refused to leave the country without him. She was doing all she could to get him released, but it wasn't clear what the charges were beyond being Jewish.

Meitner wrote to Hahn about her brother-in-law, hoping for helpful advice. Instead, she got the glib assurance that these camps weren't as brutal as people thought; such descriptions were mere rumors spread by an anti-German press. Once again, Hahn thought Meitner was overreacting. Once again, he chose not to believe newspaper articles about German oppression.

Hahn's rejection left Meitner feeling more isolated than ever. Another letter described her despair: "My very own life has the substance = zero. Unfortunately I hear very little from friends . . . and at the same time one always sits and waits longingly for news."

The news, when it came, wasn't good. In November 1938, riots swept Germany. Jewish homes and businesses were destroyed by mobs in a single night of frenzied attacks, which left hundreds of Jews dead. The destruction was called Kristallnacht, "Night of Broken Glass," because of the vast number of shattered windows. The attack was so vicious, it even made American news, though there wasn't much response after the initial gasps of horror. As the international community looked away, thousands of Jews were shipped off to concentration camps. Meitner had been appalled by the cool reaction of her colleagues to how Jews were treated in Germany, but seeing that this response was global deepened the chill in her bones. How could she feel welcome anywhere?

The physical brutality was followed by legal attacks. A new law, Atonement of the Jews, erased all civil rights for Jews. Jews had already been forced out of public schools and workplaces. Now they were barred from private institutions and businesses as well. All Jews had the name "Sara" or "Israel" added to their identity papers to make their racial ethnicity clear. Even more obvious was the yellow star they later had to sew onto their coats, clearly labeling them as Jude (German for "Jew"), warning the white Aryan public to steer clear of these undesirables. In public pronouncements, Jews were called vermin, rats, an infestation, all part of the dehumanizing propaganda to portray them as less than human.

Meitner's name was duly changed on all official documents. She was now "Lise Sara Meitner." Even in supposedly neutral Sweden, it was a reminder that wherever she went, she was marked as a Jew.

TWENTY-FIVE
AN ATOMIC MYSTERY

Even in the safety of Sweden, Meitner keenly felt the new ugly laws, the hateful language toward Jews. Her life, once so rich, felt empty without meaningful work. She felt like she was no longer a scientist. She was a Jew.
Hahn was unsympathetic, so she reached out to Elizabeth Schiemann, a biologist and one of her few women colleagues at the KWI.
"What shall I write? What the day brings me superficially has become so irrelevant and unimportant, I can't sit down and tell it. It means almost nothing to me anymore."

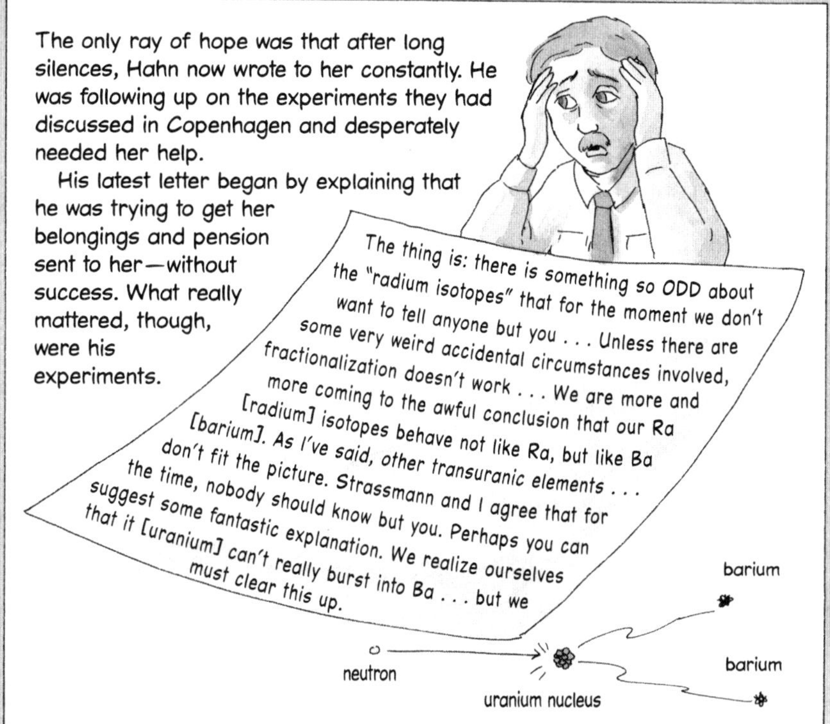
The only ray of hope was that after long silences, Hahn now wrote to her constantly. He was following up on the experiments they had discussed in Copenhagen and desperately needed her help.
His latest letter began by explaining that he was trying to get her belongings and pension sent to her—without success. What really mattered, though, were his experiments.
The thing is: there is something so ODD about the "radium isotopes" that for the moment we don't want to tell anyone but you . . . Unless there are some very weird accidental circumstances involved, fractionalization doesn't work . . . We are more and more coming to the awful conclusion that our Ra [radium] isotopes behave not like Ra, but like Ba [barium]. As I've said, other transuranic elements . . . don't fit the picture. Strassmann and I agree that for the time, nobody should know but you. Perhaps you can suggest some fantastic explanation. We realize ourselves that it [uranium] can't really burst into Ba . . . but we must clear this up.
barium
neutron
uranium nucleus
barium

Hahn was worried. He dreaded that all their research on transuranics could be wrong. Uranium was supposed to chip off heavier elements when hit with neutrons. Barium, so much lighter than uranium, made no sense at all as a result of "bursting" the element. This was why Hahn wanted to keep the results secret. Until they understood what was happening and could present a convincing interpretation, simply publishing the data would undercut their last four years of work. They would be presenting a puzzle rather than a discovery. Worse, they would be suggesting that all their earlier discoveries had been wrong.

Before Meitner could respond, Hahn ran the experiment again, determined to be extra careful and allow no possible contamination. On December 16, 1938, the same process gave the same results. It made absolutely no sense to Hahn, and he desperately pleaded with Meitner for some way to interpret the extraordinary results.

Meitner had no answer. Things didn't add up for her, either. But after Hahn had repeated the same experiment several times with great care, Meitner took the results seriously. She wrote, "We've had so many surprises in nuclear physics that one can't very well just say it is impossible." She had to figure out what this impossible thing meant. What was actually happening?

By December 22, Hahn still had no explanation from Meitner. He decided to write up the results, such as they were, leaving it to others to interpret them. He sent the paper to Rosbaud, the science editor. After describing the experiment, Hahn admitted that he and Strassmann, as chemists, had no idea how to explain the results. It was if he, like Galileo, had dropped two objects from a tower, but instead of falling, the objects had floated.

His article was scheduled to come out in January 1939. It called into question the whole line of transuranic research that he and others had been doing. He concluded: "From these experiments, we must, as chemists, rename the elements in the above scheme, and instead of radium, actinium, and thorium [the transuranics], write barium, lanthanum, and cesium. As 'nuclear chemists' who are also somewhat related to physicists, we cannot yet decide to take this big step, which contradicts all previous experience of nuclear physics. It is still possible that we could have been misled by an unusual series of accidents." Basically, he was erasing their previous work on what happened when uranium was bombarded with neutrons. What was actually being "chipped off"? Heavier elements or lighter ones? He could no longer say for sure and admitted that physicists were better positioned to understand the data, which was why he didn't take "this big step" himself.

For the December holidays, Meitner went to stay with her friend Eva in Kungälv. She loved the scenic small town on the western coast of Sweden, the perfect place to get away from the frightening news from Germany. Her nephew Otto Robert Frisch joined her, needing peace of his own as he worried about his father imprisoned in Dachau. In Kungälv, Meitner got another letter from Hahn about the puzzling results and warning her about his article coming out in January in *Die Naturwissenschaften.*

Meitner realized that something very important was happening, but it wasn't the mess Hahn thought it was. She had to understand the mystery. Walking always cleared her head, so she grabbed the letter and asked Frisch to come walk with her, she had a physics problem to untangle with him. Something very important was hidden in Hahn's confusing data, and she was determined to find it.

TWENTY-SIX

THE ATOM SPLITS!

Meitner explained to her nephew what Hahn had written.

Maybe Hahn is right— it's just a series of accidents.
People make mistakes.
No, not Hahn. Once, maybe, not over and over again. He's too precise a chemist for that.
Something else is happening.

Then Meitner saw it all in a flash. Could the nucleus have literally burst into two? They had thought that bombarding uranium with neutrons caused a "chipping away" at the atom, exposing new isotopes, the "fractionalization" and "bursting" Hahn described. Einstein had said, "There is not the slightest indication that the energy [in the nucleus] will ever be obtainable. It would mean the atom itself would have to shatter or dissolve."

What if the atom didn't shatter or dissolve? What if instead you thought of the atom like a drop of water, as Bohr suggested? A drop of water can be pulled apart until it splits. The key was the Coulomb barrier, the electrical charge holding the nucleus together, much as surface tension holds together a drop of water.

Frisch was just as excited as Meitner. He took off his skis, and the two of them sat down on a snowy log to think it all through. Meitner pulled out paper and pencil and started to do the math. Whatever was happening to the atom, its mass would be conserved since mass can't simply disappear. If the uranium atom was splitting into lighter elements, the number of protons and neutrons would still remain the same. How could uranium (atomic number 92) split into barium (atomic number 56)? That could happen only if the missing numbers were represented by krypton (atomic number 36). Then the numbers added up. Plus krypton was a gas and would have escaped without Hahn noticing.

The math looked like this:

[92u → 56Ba + 36Kr (uranium splits into barium and krypton)]

The protons 36 and 56 did add up to 92 (the atomic number for uranium), but the weight didn't add up. The mass of uranium = 238, barium = 139, krypton = 89, which meant barium and krypton only added up to 228. Where were the missing 10 units of mass?

Frisch described the moment in his autobiography: "The charge of a uranium nucleus, we found, was indeed large enough to overcome the effect of the surface tension almost completely; so the uranium nucleus might indeed resemble a very wobbly, unstable drop, ready to divide itself at the slightest provocation, such as the impact of a single neutron."

Now there was another puzzle to solve. After separation, the two drops would be driven apart by their mutual electric repulsion (the way two ends of a magnet with the same poles—negative or positive—are repelled from each other). They would gain speed and release a large amount of energy—about 200 million volts. Where would that energy come from?

From the loss of mass! That was what happened to the missing 10 units! Mass in another form was energy, as Einstein had said. Meitner had another flash of insight: As the nucleus divided, the lost mass would be transformed into energy. Einstein's theory of relativity made that clear. Using his formula of $E=mc^2$, one-fifth of a proton mass equaled 200 million electron volts—exactly the energy they had calculated. The math added up: Barium plus krypton plus the energy released equaled the atomic weight of the original uranium nucleus!

Hahn wasn't seeing a strange new superlight transuranic. He was seeing the atom being split. And he was seeing an incredibly powerful source of energy. He just didn't know what he was looking at.

So many experiments had been done bombarding atoms—by Bohr, Fermi, and others. Why hadn't this happened before?

The answer, Meitner saw, was that it had. They'd all been splitting atoms. But they hadn't known it. They didn't think it was possible, so they hadn't realized what was happening right in front of them.

To be fair, Frisch later suggested, there was a reason for this. They weren't being stupid. It was just that the amounts of energy being released were so small, they weren't noticed. And everyone had been looking at these experiments in terms of chemistry, not physics.

Mostly, though, Meitner admitted that "we had been blinded by 'the rules.' The atom could never be split, we believed, so we didn't have the . . . courage to see the opposite even when it was staring us in the face, even when no other solution would fit."

It was a solution that held huge potential—and dangers.

TWENTY-SEVEN

THE IMPOSSIBLE IS POSSIBLE!

Einstein wrote about the discovery in his autobiography, giving Meitner full credit for grasping not only that nuclear fission could happen but how it happened.

I believed only that it was theoretically possible . . . It was discovered by Hahn in Berlin, and he himself misinterpreted what he discovered. It was Lise Meitner who provided the correct interpretation.

Hahn had done the experiments, but Meitner understood their meaning. Together they had discovered that atoms could split. This science became the basis for nuclear energy and weapons.

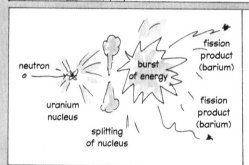

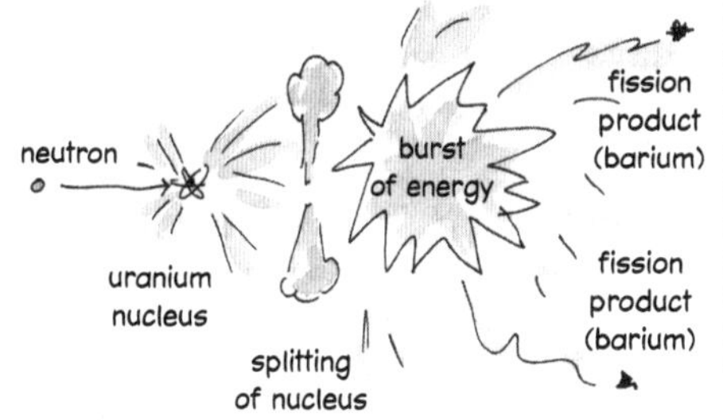
neutron
uranium nucleus
splitting of nucleus
burst of energy
fission product (barium)
fission product (barium)

Meitner understood the implications but had no idea how realistic they were. All she knew for sure was that the world's understanding of the atom was about to change dramatically. This was big, as big as $E=mc^2$.

Meitner wrote to Hahn after Christmas but didn't tell him her interpretation yet. She needed to wait for Frisch to return to Copenhagen and run his own experiments to validate their theory. She cautioned Hahn not to present his findings as an oddity, then wrote a few days later, briefly outlining the possibility that the nucleus had divided. Meanwhile, Frisch rushed back to Copenhagen to tell Niels Bohr.

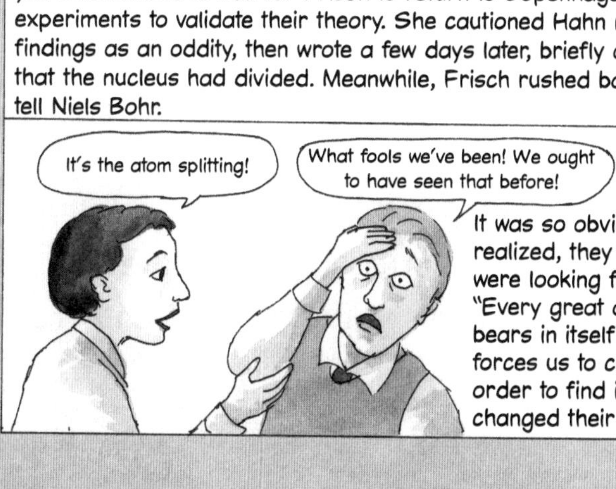
It's the atom splitting!
What fools we've been! We ought to have seen that before!

It was so obvious, but as Meitner realized, they only saw what they were looking for. As Bohr said, "Every great and deep difficulty bears in itself its own solution. It forces us to change our thinking in order to find it." Meitner had changed their thinking.

Bohr was as excited as Frisch, but he also wanted to be sure that Meitner and her nephew got the credit they deserved for this revolutionary discovery. Bohr urged Frisch to publish their ideas as soon as possible. Frisch called his aunt, and they agreed he would write a quick draft to send to *Nature*, the international science journal that could publish most quickly. He sent her his report in a few days, calling the split "fission," a term he borrowed from a biologist colleague who described cell division that way. Meitner agreed with the coinage and edited the paper, and they submitted it to *Nature* as "A New Type of Nuclear Reaction."

While waiting for publication, Frisch replicated Hahn's experiment and saw with his own eyes the truth of their theory. He sent a brief note to *Nature* as a follow-up to their report on the new splitting of the atom, "Physical Evidence of the Division of Heavy Nuclei under Neutron Bombardment."

On January 14, before the *Nature* publication, Meitner finally wrote a complete interpretation of the troubling experiments and sent it to Hahn. She wanted him to know that he would see her articles in *Nature*. Her name would be on a major discovery, perhaps *the* discovery of the twentieth century. And this time her name came first: Lise Meitner. Her nephew's name came second, and in a fitting kind of justice, using only his initials, O. R. Frisch.

Meitner explained to Hahn precisely what the experiments meant—not the discovery of new light isotopes, but a rupture of the uranium nucleus. She added, "I have totally retracted my [earlier transuranic] paper as of 14 days ago . . . Since, in fact, I no longer believe in the earlier interpretation of our experiments, and I of course don't want it published, even in the odd annual publication. The new explanation is also more beautiful and much more clearly comprehensible; it really is a wonderful thing."

While Meitner and Frisch were writing up their ideas, Bohr had been on a ship to the United States, heading for the Fifth Washington Conference on Theoretical Physics. He had done the same calculations Meitner and Frisch had done on that snowy day in Kungälv. He got off the ship and was met by his old friend Enrico Fermi. Fermi had started the experiments on transuranics (in fact, that work was what had earned him the Nobel Prize). Bohr told him about Meitner's incredible work. The two scientists agreed to announce the revolutionary news themselves, giving clear credit to Lise Meitner and Otto Robert Frisch. They would be speaking to the top physicists in the world at the conference. What better place to announce such a momentous discovery?

Right after the opening remarks on January 26, 1939, Bohr went onstage and announced that Otto Hahn and Fritz Strassmann in Berlin-Dahlem had radiochemical confirmation that bombarding uranium with slow neutrons resulted in barium. Lise Meitner and Otto Robert Frisch had interpreted these results as the splitting of the uranium nucleus, releasing much energy.

The short speech electrified the crowd. Reporters assigned to the conference didn't understand why scientists were suddenly rushing out of the hall, eager to test the results for themselves or to call home to their labs and have colleagues duplicate the experiment. The daily newspapers reported "Bohr's exciting news," without grasping what it meant. Some journalists didn't even get basic facts right, identifying Otto Robert Frisch as Niels Bohr's son-in-law, rather than as a researcher working at his lab.

The moment was so historic, a commemorative plaque was later put up outside the room where Bohr made his speech, room 209 in the Hall of Government at George Washington University. The important names listed on the plaque don't include Meitner or Frisch—exactly what Bohr had hoped to avoid.

Meitner and Frisch's article appeared two weeks later, on February 11, 1939. It concluded: "It seems therefore possible that the uranium nucleus has only small stability of form, and may, after neutron capture, divide itself into two nuclei of roughly equal size." Just in time for this, Meitner's lab in Stockholm was ready, and she could, like her nephew, see the evidence with her own eyes. At last, she felt like a physicist again! She submitted a quick follow-up of her own to *Nature*, "New Products of the Fission of the Thorium Nucleus."

Before Meitner and Frisch's discovery, the idea of harnessing atomic energy was considered a pipe dream, something for science fiction writers, not real scientists. In 1933, Ernest Rutherford, the British physicist who had discovered the nucleus, wrote, "Anyone who says that with the means at present at our disposal and our present knowledge we can utilize atomic energy is talking moonshine." In the years that followed, great strides were made in understanding protons, neutrons, the model of the atom, and how it behaved, but atomic fission remained beyond imagining. By 1936, Bohr felt that harvesting atomic energy was less and less likely. "The more our knowledge of nuclear reactions advances the remoter this goal [of harnessing energy] seems to become." Other scientists saw it as theoretically possible but practically impossible. Once radiation was seen as coming from within the atom, it was obvious that it held great energy. But how to release it and—more importantly—control it? These problems seemed insurmountable.

Until Meitner's discovery. The incredible had happened—the question now was what next? Word of nuclear fission spread quickly, and the original experiments were replicated in America and Britain. By early February 1939, even the general public knew of the achievement. *Time* magazine wrote, "Last week the Hahn report reached the U.S. and physicists sprang to their laboratories to see whether they could confirm it. Early this week the physics laboratories of Columbia and Johns Hopkins Universities, and of the Carnegie Institution of Washington, announced full confirmation." Again, no mention was made of Meitner or Frisch.

In the flurry of excitement, their role was forgotten. Hahn's name was still mentioned, but Meitner's slipped away.

Meitner felt invisible once again. She wrote to Hahn:

> I don't feel at all happy. Here I just have a workplace, no position that would entitle me to anything.

> Try to imagine what it would be like if, instead of your nice private institute, you had a room in an institute which is not your own, without any help, without any rights, and with the attitude of Siegbahn who only loves big machines [the cyclotron] and who is very confident and self-assured—and there am I with my inner shyness and embarrassment! And that I have to do all the petty work which I haven't done for 20 years. Of course, it's my fault. I should have prepared my departure much better and much earlier, I should at least have had drawings of the most important apparatus, etc. . . . But the essential thing is that I have come here so empty-handed. Now Siegbahn will soon believe—especially after your excellent results—that I didn't do anything and that you both did all the physics too at Berlin-Dahlem. I am losing all my courage.

Meitner was begging Hahn to give her credit for her interpretation. He, of course, had done none of the physics. He had no inkling of the enormity of his experiments, no understanding of atomic structure. But he couldn't admit that Meitner had guided his experiments, that she had been as much a part of the work as he himself. He could not afford to have his name professionally linked to a Jew's. Over and over again, he thought Meitner should have understood that and not asked so much of him. After all, he was still trying to get her furniture and library shipped to her. Wasn't that enough?

He wrote a terse letter back, insisting that *his* discovery "owed nothing to physics!" He conveniently forgot that his own article had left the interpretation to physicists, admitting chemists couldn't understand the data. He had no idea that Meitner's thinking was based on quantum physics, on Einstein's famous formula of the relationship between energy and mass.

The lack of support in Stockholm, along with Hahn's cold shoulder, was too much for Meitner. She took the train and ferry to Copenhagen, to Niels Bohr's institute, where she always felt warmly welcomed. Bohr was still in America, but Frisch was there, plus a well-equipped lab where she could see atoms being split for herself. As each neutron smashed into a uranium nucleus, a great burst of energy–vibrating green lines–flashed on the fluorescent screen attached to her apparatus.

It was thrilling and beautiful and true–everything Boltzmann had said about physics so long ago.

TWENTY-EIGHT

THE POWER OF NUCLEAR FISSION

From Niels Bohr's institute, Meitner wrote to Hahn, reproaching him for taking sole credit for the work they'd done together. Now she wrote papers with Frisch, showing that "transuranics" were actually products of nuclear fission that had been misunderstood.

But Meitner missed a major implication of her "beautiful theory." A single split atom released a small amount of energy. But what if a chain reaction happened, where one split atom produced neutrons that would split another and another and another until . . .

The energy released would be enormous, like a small sun exploding. It could create a bomb more powerful than any ever imagined.

Leo Szilard, Meitner's old teaching partner, was afraid of exactly that happening. He warned Fermi.

We need to keep any work on a chain reaction secret!
Nuts!
It's a theory—it couldn't really happen. Scientists are supposed to share information.
Not with the Nazis!
It's more science fiction than science!

September 1, 1939: Hitler invaded Poland. France and Britain responded by declaring war on Germany. It was the start of World War II, and the idea of Germany gaining a superbomb was terrifying. Allied scientists agreed to work in secret.

Rosbaud, the science editor and Meitner's friend who had helped her in her escape from Berlin, found himself in a pivotal position. He traveled all over the world, talking to scientists and inviting them to write for his journal. He knew what everyone was working on. With the discovery of nuclear fission, he had an even bigger task as a spy. He needed to learn as much as he could about the Nazis' nuclear research. If Hitler got close to making an atomic bomb, the world needed to know.

Meitner was central to all this. She passed on news she got from Hahn and other German scientists visiting neutral Sweden. She gave books and information to Rosbaud and others working with the Allies. One of her contacts was Moe Berg, a Jewish American baseball player turned spy, looking for information on resistance fighters and nuclear scientists. When Meitner wanted to get a letter to Hahn, Berg often delivered it, and he was a regular go-between with Rosbaud as well.

Was Meitner even aware of the possibility of an atomic bomb? In the fall of 1939, she was more focused on her "beautiful" discovery and the way she had been ignored. The 1939 Nobel

Prize in Physics went to Ernest Lawrence at the University of California, Berkeley, for the development of the cyclotron. Meitner's discovery was vastly more important, but Siegbahn, on the Nobel committee, loved big machines and was no fan of Meitner, even though she worked at his institute. Meitner and Hahn had both been nominated for the Nobel Prize in Chemistry for their work on nuclear fission, but the committee gave the prize to two others for separate research. And in 1940–42, there was no Nobel Prize in Chemistry at all, due to "political instability." That meant the committee wanted to give the prize to German scientists, but Hitler had forbidden German citizens from accepting any Nobel awards after the 1935 Nobel Peace Prize was given to Carl von Ossietzky. He was a German pacifist who had been convicted of high treason for exposing German rearmament after World War I. Ironically, Hitler himself was nominated for the Nobel Peace Prize in 1939 (by a member of the Swedish parliament). Instead, no peace prize was given at all that year.

Hearing that she had been passed over by the Nobel committees, Meitner despaired. In late 1939, soon after the start of World War II, she wrote to Hahn that "my work is equivalent to zero." She felt at the lowest point of her career. Hahn's letters remained cold and formal, complaining about the difficulties of working during a war, but Meitner kept on writing to him. She asked about his family, worried about wartime shortages, and hoped for a crumb of concern to be shown to her.

There was some good news in the middle of all the bleakness. Meitner's brother-in-law, Frisch's father, was freed from Dachau. He and his wife joined Meitner in Sweden. Meitner's other sisters and brothers got out of Austria as well, finding safety in the United States.

Frisch also moved. He had been worried for a while that Copenhagen wasn't safe from invasion by Hitler. When he told a fellow Jewish physicist, George Placzek, about his fears, Placzek retorted, "Why should Hitler occupy Denmark? He can just telephone, can't he?"

The bitter observation wasn't reassuring. Placzek himself decided to leave (and ended up the only one of his entire extended family to survive the Nazi Holocaust). Frisch followed. He was on a trip to England when war against Germany was officially declared. Instead of returning to Copenhagen, Frisch managed to get a position at the University of Birmingham in England, where he met Rudolf Peierls, another German émigré scientist. The two physicists were ostracized as "enemy aliens." Both were Jewish refugees fleeing the Nazis, but to the British, they were suspicious Germans, possibly spies. Although they were allowed to work together, their movements were strictly controlled, and they were held to a tight curfew.

Frisch and Peierls were following up the implications of nuclear fission. Could such energy be harnessed into a weapon? At first, it seemed that far too much uranium would be needed to generate a big blast. But Frisch and Peierls figured out that if instead of using the more common uranium-238, they separated out the rarer form of uranium-235, a much smaller amount would be needed for a critical mass. It wasn't a matter of tons of uranium, as most had thought, but of only a few pounds. A conventional detonator could then set off a tremendously powerful explosion. They wrote up this first technical description of an atomic bomb in the Frisch-Peierls memorandum, the document that made Britain and the United States take seriously the risk of Germany developing a superweapon. This wasn't something they shared widely, only letting British scientists know about the risk. Szilard, working on nuclear fission at Columbia University, was still warning physicists about the danger of Nazi scientists following the same research.

The British top scientific priority was to develop radar to track the German submarines, airplanes, and later rockets bombarding their country. Those curious about nuclear power considered it highly unlikely that atomic energy could ever be generated in meaningful amounts. The Germans also thought atomic energy improbable in the near future, concentrating instead on long-range missiles to attack England–and beyond. While the top British scientists worked on radar, the best German ones worked on missiles, two sides of the same problem. Only a small group in Germany, led by Werner Heisenberg, focused on nuclear power. Hahn was part of Heisenberg's group.

In 1936, Heisenberg had been condemned by the SS as a "white Jew," that is, an Aryan who sympathized with Jews, because of his work in quantum physics, the so-called depraved Jewish science. A thorough investigation by the SS followed. Heisenberg, a loyal German, appealed to Heinrich Himmler, the head of the SS, to clear his name. It took two years, but in 1938, Himmler intervened on Heisenberg's behalf, arguing that Germany couldn't afford to lose the Nobel Prize–winning physicist. Heisenberg was needed to educate and train future German scientists. The SS report on Heisenberg admitted that he followed the "Jewish" school of physics, but "he is ready at any time to defend Germany whole-heartedly . . . he is of the opinion that you are either 'born a good German or not' . . . Today Heisenberg also rejects in principle the infiltration of foreign Jewish influence into the German living space."

His credibility as a staunch Jew-hater restored, Heisenberg

was a leading member of what was called the Uranium Group, researching nuclear fission for the Reich, though far more support went into missile work.

Szilard wasn't taking any chances. He had to make sure that Germany never developed an atomic weapon. He had run his own experiments after Bohr's explosive announcement. Szilard knew that a chain reaction was possible. A weapon of horrific power could be made from fissioning uranium. Szilard didn't have any influence on politicians himself, but he was friends with a physicist whose opinion meant a lot—Albert Einstein. With the help of fellow Jewish Hungarian émigrés Eugene Wigner and Edward Teller, Szilard drafted a letter addressed to President Franklin D. Roosevelt for Einstein to sign. The letter warned the American president about the very real potential for Germany to make a doomsday machine. The only solution was for the United States to do it first.

TWENTY-NINE

A LETTER FROM EINSTEIN

Szilard tracked down Einstein, on vacation in Long Island, New York, and got right to the point.

You realize what's at stake now? The atom has not only been split, a chain reaction could trigger a giant atomic explosion.
I never thought of that!

The risk was so great that Einstein was willing to sound the alarm, even if it turned out the Germans weren't following this line of research. As Szilard noted, "The one thing that most scientists are really afraid of is to make a fool of themselves. Einstein was free of such fear and this above all is what made his position unique on this occasion."

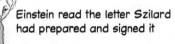

Einstein read the letter Szilard had prepared and signed it

The letter went on to warn that the best sources of uranium (in the Congo and Czechoslovakia) could easily fall into German hands and noted that Germany had already stopped the sale of uranium from any mines that it controlled. This ominously suggested that the Nazis were already working on developing such mega-bombs. Otherwise, why bother with uranium?

The letter outlined steps the Roosevelt administration could take to outrace the German scientists, including staying in close touch with American physicists and their atomic work. More than that, the letter recommended that the president "speed up the experimental work, which is at present being carried on within the limits of the budgets of University laboratories, by providing funds . . . and perhaps also by obtaining the co-operation of industrial laboratories which have the necessary equipment."

Physicists were warning the British government as well about the military potential of this new science. Nuclear fission could generate incredible energy, but it could also be used for the biggest bomb the world had ever seen. What would happen if Germany developed such a weapon?

The Frisch-Peierls memorandum outlined how to sustain a nuclear reaction and showed that the bomb wouldn't need to be as heavy as Einstein thought. Their research led to the Tube Alloys Project, the code name for a secret British program to develop a nuclear weapon. Frisch and Peierls were invited to be part of this top secret project (despite their enemy alien status) and sent to Liverpool, where a cyclotron would help them test their ideas.

Einstein's suggestions became the seeds for the Manhattan Project, the vast American effort to build a nuclear weapon. Britain had nowhere near the resources of the United States, and once the Manhattan Project was started, the Tube Alloys Project became part of the much bigger American venture. While the United States ended up employing 130,000 people and spending 2 billion dollars on the project, Germany's Ministry of War set up a small office for nuclear research with nowhere near the personnel, funding, or organization. Heisenberg lobbied for more money from the government but was told the work was too speculative to be worth much investment. German censorship also hindered their progress. German physicists could no longer read international science news. And

Meitner, Hahn's contact in neutral Sweden, wasn't sharing any information. She was now too wary of Hahn to write about atomic work. Their partnership was definitely over, though she tried to keep some kind of friendship alive. Her letters now focused on daily life, her despair, and his worries.

For a long time, Meitner didn't have her furniture, her books, or her equipment. When her possessions were finally delivered, in May 1939, everything was broken and torn, crated hastily in a showy mess. Very little was salvageable. She wrote Hahn, "In two weeks it won't seem important, but right now it makes me feel pretty low." Meitner sat, surrounded by the scraps of her former life. There was no way to put together the pieces again.

THIRTY

THE RACE FOR THE BOMB

April 9, 1940: *Germany invaded Denmark.* Meitner had just arrived in Copenhagen, staying at the institute. Bohr was on a night ferry from Oslo, Norway, and she nervously waited for him, worried the boat would be sunk.

Meitner wrote a friend: "We were all much relieved, as you may imagine, when [Niels] came. We had been awakened by the noise of plenty of aeroplanes at about a quarter to six in the morning and there was nothing to do but await what might happen next. The central post office, the offices of the newspapers, radio stations, and police stations were occupied almost immediately, but you saw very few soldiers on the street . . . They did not interfere officially with anything so long as I was there . . . Of course, Niels and Margrethe are very unhappy . . . But he doesn't have it in view to give up his work."

Bohr and his institute may have been safe, but Meitner wasn't. She hid in the institute for weeks until Bohr figured out a way to sneak her onto a fishing boat back to Sweden.

Once again, Meitner had to cross a border, escaping the Nazis. This time, though, she was just as worried about Bohr being left behind as about herself going.

Once back in Stockholm, Meitner shared the news the scientific world was waiting for: What had happened to Bohr in Nazi-occupied Copenhagen? Had the Gestapo arrested him? She sent a telegram to a friend in England:

MET NIELS AND MARGRETHE RECENTLY BOTH WELL BUT UNHAPPY ABOUT EVENTS PLEASE INFORM COCKCROFT AND MAUD RAY KENT.

John Cockcroft was a British physicist working on radar, hoping to develop a device small enough to fit in a plane's cockpit so pilots could see enemy planes approaching. He was also part of the Tube Alloys Project to investigate nuclear power and one of Meitner's contacts getting information on German nuclear work. Cockcroft was alarmed by the message. He couldn't figure out what Meitner was trying to tell him in this strange new code. The whole committee tried to decipher it. James Chadwick, the physicist who had discovered the neutron, thought it was a warning about a German death ray.

Cockcroft thought the odd words "MAUD RAY KENT" could be a near anagram for "RADIUM TAKEN." A cryptographer read it as "MAKE UR DAY NT." In honor of the puzzle, the scientists named the nuclear investigation committee the MAUD Committee.

The mystery was solved when Wilfrid Basil Mann joined the MAUD Committee. He had met the real Maud Ray. She had been the governess for the Bohr family and now lived in Kent. Meitner's message had been exactly what it seemed–no secret code, just "let people know the Bohr family is okay."

At least for a while. Bohr would need to escape Copenhagen as Meitner had, since his mother was Jewish. But in 1940, Bohr felt he could still stay at his laboratories.

A month later, it was France's turn to face the German onslaught. Again a quick invasion, followed by occupation. The same was true for the Netherlands and Belgium, both invaded when France was. It looked like Hitler would rule all of Europe. And he was doing this with conventional warfare. What would happen if he had a superbomb?

Despite the tight tabs Germany kept on its scientists, Hahn managed to get a lecture trip to London approved before the invasions closed off all travel. He would be accompanied by a Nazi minder who would make sure he didn't spill any German secrets. Instead, Hahn should see what he could learn from his fellow scientists there.

Meitner wrote ahead to her brother Walter and her nephew Otto Frisch to be wary of Hahn. He was not "completely free because of a colleague [the minder]. And perhaps inwardly he is also not completely free." This last sentence shows that Meitner had given up on Hahn. He would never stand up for her, never stand up for any of his Jewish colleagues. And he would never admit her role in what he now considered "his" impressive discovery. He may not have been an official member of the Nazi party, but Meitner considered him completely complicit in all of its policies.

THIRTY-ONE

A LAB OF ONE'S OWN

December 7, 1941: The Japanese attacked Pearl Harbor in Hawaii, inflicting massive damage on the U.S. naval fleet stationed there. The United States entered the war, fighting Japan, Germany, and Italy (the Axis powers).

Although Hitler had invaded Norway, on the same date as the invasion of Denmark, Sweden (like Switzerland to the south) remained neutral. Sweden allowed Germany to transport equipment and soldiers through their land to occupy Norway. Soon Germany was fighting on all fronts, including against Britain and, from mid-1941, the Soviet Union. A superweapon would be very useful.

Around this charged time, the Reich's minister of armaments and munitions, Albert Speer, met with Heisenberg to talk about making a nuclear bomb. Heisenberg admitted it was theoretically possible but technically too difficult to try. It would take years with maximum support from the government.

Speer wrote after the war:

> Hitler had sometimes spoken to me about the possibility of an atomic bomb, but the idea quite obviously strained his intellectual capacity. He was also unable to grasp the revolutionary nature of nuclear physics. In the 2,200 written points of references from my conferences with Hitler, nuclear fission comes up only once, and then it is mentioned with extreme brevity. Actually, Professor Heisenberg had not given any final answer to my question whether a successful nuclear fission could be kept under control with absolute certainty or might continue as a chain reaction. I am sure Hitler would

> have not hesitated for a moment to employ atom bombs against England.

Heisenberg focused instead on building a "uranium engine," a nuclear reactor to provide power. Even at this, though, he didn't get very far. Hahn was on his team, but the major German physicists had left the country, a brain drain created by the Nazis. Instead, this elite Jewish scientific talent was working for the Allies.

In mid-September 1941, Heisenberg visited Bohr's institute in Copenhagen. Bohr feared that Heisenberg was the lead scientist building a Nazi superbomb. Was he coming to Copenhagen as a spy, to discover how the Allies were progressing on their own atomic weapon? Was he planning to steal Bohr's research?

Heisenberg acted as if there was nothing wrong with Germany occupying Denmark. He proudly showed Bohr the diagram of a reactor to produce plutonium, the work his group was doing in Germany. Then he asked about atomic bombs, trying to get a sense of what kind of work was being done in other countries. Bohr revealed nothing, horrified by Heisenberg's calm acceptance of fascism. Heisenberg ignored his old friend's awkward silences. He kept probing for information while bragging that Germany would win the war and that a nuclear weapon could be a decisive part of that victory. At least, this was Bohr's report of events, written to Meitner shortly after the visit.

Heisenberg told a different story. He described warning of the immorality of using nuclear weapons and how that weighed on scientists, suggesting they should be careful what they developed. Heisenberg presented this version after the war as evidence that he had never intended to make an atomic weapon. He insisted that he had the moral scruples to choose not to pursue it, while Bohr had no such ethics.

Meitner described the now famous meeting in a letter to her old friend from the KWI, Max von Laue: "Half amusing and half depressing was his [Bohr's] report about a visit of Werner [Heisenberg] and Carl Friedrich [von Weizsäcker] . . . but I beg you to keep this confidential. I became very melancholy on hearing this; at one time I had held them to be decent human beings. They have gone astray." Meitner would never forgive either man for their complicity with the Nazis. She was especially angry at Heisenberg for pretending to hold the high moral ground and considered his visit to Copenhagen a spy mission that was "unforgivable."

If Heisenberg was indeed trying to get information from Bohr about the status of an atomic weapon, he came away no wiser. But Bohr took the bluff seriously. He respected Heisenberg too much as a scientist. If Heisenberg thought Germany would win the war, the Allies had something serious to worry about. Meitner was equally anxious. She told Njål Hole, a nuclear physicist and chemical engineer and her contact in the Norwegian resistance, "I am afraid that the Allies have no man such as Heisenberg."

The two weren't alone in their fears. The idea of a nuclear bomb was no longer abstract theory but something the Allies were determined to build before the Germans. Work on the Manhattan Project ramped up. Both Frisch and Peierls, the supposedly suspicious "enemy aliens," were quickly made British citizens and sent to Los Alamos, New Mexico, to work on the Manhattan Project.

As the person who had discovered nuclear fission, Meitner was offered a position alongside her nephew. She was tempted by the thought of a well-equipped lab with an organization solidly supporting her work. But she was horrified by the idea of working on anything that could be used as a weapon. She had detested Hahn's role in chemical warfare in World War I. She wouldn't be part of anything that promised to be many times worse. She refused, saying, "I will have nothing to do with a bomb!" She wanted to stop the Nazis any way she could—except by developing a superweapon. For her, physics had always been about truth, not power, about understanding the world, not manipulating it. Scientists had a responsibility to be aware of the moral implications of their work. Meitner supported harnessing atomic energy to light homes or power machines, but she was horrified by the idea of using that energy for great destruction. She had never intended her discovery to lead to such a nightmare.

While the Allies rushed to build the bomb, the Germans had decided such a thing was unlikely. In January 1942, the new president of the Kaiser Wilhelm Society, an ardent Nazi named Dr. Albert Vögler, and General Emil Leeb, the head of the German army's Weapons Research Office, met in Berlin to discuss a nuclear future. Leeb was satisfied with the weapons the Reich was already using. He saw no need for some exotic, pie-in-the-sky bomb and argued that researching nuclear power for producing electricity had already been explored enough. Uranium research belonged on the back burner, something to look at later, definitely not essential to the war effort. Vögler didn't agree and pressed Albert Speer for some form of support for atomic research.

Speer met again with Heisenberg and his group, including Hahn. He listened to their complaints about weak funding and passed on the message to Hitler, a second chance to rethink atomic studies. But Hitler had just received a report on exactly this subject from his photographer, Heinrich Hoffmann, denying the need for any more support. Speer wrote, "It is significant that Hitler did not choose the direct route of obtaining information on this matter from responsible people but depended instead on unreliable and incompetent informants to give him a Sunday-supplement account. Here again was proof of his love for amateurishness and his lack of understanding of fundamental scientific research."

Hahn still had his lab, still had his research position and his comfortable salary, but this wasn't a happy time for him. He felt marginalized. Now he was the one complaining to Meitner about being ignored rather than the other way around. The important scientists were working on rockets. That work had all the attention, money, and glory–and no need for chemists specializing in radioactivity. The early excitement over Hahn's major discovery of atomic fission had fizzled away. He expected Meitner to commiserate with him. Instead, she avoided the topic completely.

THIRTY-TWO

ANOTHER PHYSICIST ESCAPES

By September 1943, Bohr's name was on the *Gestapo's* list, because his mother was Jewish. It was time to leave Denmark. First, he cleared the institute of all records about nuclear work and Jewish refugee scientists, and then Bohr and his family sneaked out the way Meitner had, on small fishing boats.
To keep valuable equipment out of Nazi hands, the Danish underground rigged the institute with explosives. But Heisenberg came, looked around, and left. So instead of blowing up the institute, the underground let it be abandoned.
In Stockholm, Meitner rushed to meet Bohr, but he didn't want to rest. He wanted to see the Swedish king.
He has to save the Danish Jews!
I must convince him!
Hitler has said that welcoming refugees would be 'unjustifiable interference in the affairs of Germany.'
What about interfering in *Danish* affairs?
Sigh!
But that night, the king gave a special radio broadcast.
ALL DANISH REFUGEES ARE WELCOME IN SWEDEN.
The Danish underground mobilized a fleet of fishing boats, smuggling Jewish families across the icy sea. Some boats were intercepted by the Nazis, but most landed safely, rescuing more than 6,000 Jews.

Meitner was anguished by what was happening to Jews all over Europe. She didn't feel herself to be particularly Jewish, but she didn't understand how any human wouldn't be appalled by the Nazis' brutality.

Bohr didn't think of himself as Jewish, either. But he couldn't stand by as Germany occupied Europe. It was time for him to join the race to build the atomic bomb. He respected Meitner's position. He also didn't want to build a death machine. But Hitler had to be stopped. And for Bohr that meant joining the Manhattan Project.

A British bomber plane was sent to pick up Bohr from Stockholm and bring him to London. From there, he would make his way to Los Alamos. Eventually, his family would follow. But first the pilot had to cross the enemy airspace of Nazi-occupied Norway. He flew a zigzag course to avoid being shot down and landed safely in London. Safely for him, at least. Bohr, in the back cargo bay, had passed out from the altitude. His head was too big for the helmet the pilot had handed him, so he hadn't worn it, and he hadn't heard the instructions to turn on his oxygen supply.

Fortunately, he wasn't seriously hurt. Once he came to, his first worry was to make sure the Tube Alloys Project knew about the German atomic efforts, the ones Heisenberg had boasted about. He didn't know the real status of the project, only his worst fears. Then Bohr went on to New Mexico. Major General Leslie Groves, who directed the Manhattan Project, described Bohr's impact in his memoir about it:

"He came at the right moment. The exigencies of the production, the innumerable small problems which confronted the physicists, had led them away from some of the fundamental problems of the bomb. The study of the fission process itself had been neglected . . . Here Bohr's interest gave rise to new theoretical and experimental activities which cleared up many questions that were left unanswered before."

At its height, the Manhattan Project was spread out in three cities: Oak Ridge in Tennessee, Hanford in Washington State, and Los Alamos in New Mexico. From New Mexico, Bohr sent cryptic messages to his wife and Meitner, not able to tell them anything meaningful. Now Meitner had two people writing to her from Los Alamos, Bohr and Frisch, neither of whom could really say anything about their work. Which only made her feel more left out.

Her world felt emptier than ever. But she couldn't, she wouldn't, help build a bomb.

THIRTY-THREE

THE GERMAN NUCLEAR PROGRAM

Meitner heard little news now from Britain and America. The only easy contact she had was with Germany. The Nazis admired the neutral Swedes as perfect Aryans—tall, blond, and blue-eyed. German scientists often came to Stockholm.

Which made Meitner pivotal for gathering scientific information. Rosbaud relied on her passing on the news she got from her visitors. She also handed over technical books, notes, and coded books passed on by Norwegian physicists working for British intelligence.

Knowing everyone, yet being seen as an insignificant woman, nobody suspected Meitner.

How is Berlin these days?
You should be glad to be here! You opened a big can of worms with your atomic fission idea and now we're scrambling to figure it out. I'll leave you my notes. Tell me what you think.

I'll have to describe this delicious wine to dear Lise! You wouldn't know there was a war on.
Luckily rationing isn't for us.
The Reich needs our brilliant minds, after all. We'll make a powerful nuclear engine, you'll see.
In your dreams! As soon as we solve one problem, another pops up. It's impossible!

One of Meitner's major sources was Max von Laue, an old friend from the KWI. He wrote to her about his regular dinners with colleagues, sharing all the scientific gossip they enjoyed over lavish meals. As long as he said nothing political, he felt free to write long letters.

When Meitner heard again from Hahn, he reported that nuclear fission gave them a choice between a "super-explosive" or a "uranium machine." He told her that he chose the uranium machine (a nuclear reactor for energy production) as the easier to build and the safer option. Heisenberg agreed and presented this to Hitler. The nuclear program was stepped up, though still underfunded compared to missile research. This news was passed on to Rosbaud.

A couple of months later, Hahn came to Stockholm to lecture on nuclear fission. He wanted to see Meitner, confident that there were no hard feelings between them, and suggested they celebrate her sixty-fifth birthday together. Meitner was happy to see Hahn, too, to get back a small taste of the life of scientific exploration they had once shared. But she was disappointed that he still couldn't admit her role in the discovery of nuclear fission, still couldn't acknowledge what the Nazis were doing to Jews. The things left unsaid created an awkward distance.

Hahn's lecture was the opposite of what Meitner had heard

from Bohr and her nephew, though she didn't tell Hahn that. Hahn described the enormous potential of a nuclear chain reaction but ended his talk with doubts that "it was possible to surmount the technical difficulties involved." He didn't know that Frisch and Peierls had already solved two of the technical problems—the amount of uranium needed and how to sustain a chain reaction. He didn't know about the Manhattan Project. All he knew was that the German government had given up on an atomic weapon. He assumed everyone else had as well. Meitner wasn't going to give any hint otherwise, and now she had another reassuring message to send to Bohr. And to Rosbaud.

Rosbaud knew from his own conversations what Meitner was now confirming: Heisenberg's group was having only minor success with their "uranium machine." This news, though, didn't slow the pace at Los Alamos. Germany was too much of a scientific powerhouse to be underestimated.

The Allies pounded Berlin with bombs. The KWI was hit in February 1944, and to clean up the rubble, the Nazis brought in concentration camp prisoners. The weakened, starving men were forced to work long hours. Rosbaud, still living in Berlin, came to help clear debris and gave the gaunt prisoners fresh rolls to eat. Even a crust of bread given to a Jew was a criminal act. But Rosbaud took the risk. One of Hahn's coworkers noticed the dangerous gift, remembering it years later: "This courageous deed made a deep impression on the young people. We would not have dared to do it."

Hahn wrote bitter, angry letters to Meitner about the bombings. He would later claim he had no idea of the deprivations in the camps, though he saw the skeletal prisoners himself. He was too focused on his own losses to think about anyone else. Hahn and his fellow scientists were moved to Tailfingen in the south. From safety there, Hahn complained about the Allies targeting a scholarly institute. Why not bomb munitions, rocket bases, railroad depots, he asked, making no mention of any camps or prisoners. Meitner, forgetting all the times Hahn had called her bitter and angry, tried to console her old partner.

Hahn's next letter was anguished for a different reason. He wrote to Meitner that the SS was pressuring Hitler to force the Uranium Group to make an atomic bomb. The scientists didn't think that was possible, but they were being ignored. Hahn dreaded having to work for the SS. But he couldn't refuse. Another message Meitner gave to Rosbaud.

Speer, who wrote so much about Hitler and his attitude toward science, didn't say a word about this shift. For him, the atomic effort had its last chance at a meeting on June 4, 1942. It died when Heisenberg gave a weak presentation about nuclear possibilities and asked for such a small sum that it was impossible to take the effort seriously. The Luftwaffe, the German air force, was then spending roughly 2 billion dollars every three months on its new technology (about the same cost as the entire Manhattan Project). Speer, a believer in an atomic bomb despite Heisenberg's lukewarm attitude, offered the scientist a few million marks to ramp up the work, and General Fromm agreed to lend several hundred scientists from military duty to help with the project. Heisenberg's answer was that he had no idea how to use such vast resources. That was the end of any real work on a nuclear weapon or nuclear power reactor. But hearing rumors of mass murder in the concentration camps, Meitner wasn't reassured. The Nazis seemed capable of killing vast numbers even without a superbomb.

THIRTY-FOUR

WHAT TO DO WITH NAZI SCIENTISTS?

With America in the war, the Allies were finally winning. Plans were made for what would happen next. The Nazis were sure to have a treasure trove of secret weapons. The plan for the Alsos Mission was hatched: Special agents would follow the troops and track down scientific information—and the scientists themselves.

D-Day, June 6, 1944: The Allies landed on the French beaches of Normandy.

Chemical teams came, too, in case the Germans used new radioactive weapons. It turned out to be old-fashioned warfare—guns, mines, bombs. It was still deadly, with 10,000 soldiers killed and wounded, but the Allies gradually swept beyond the beaches, through France, and into Germany. Alsos followed, finding German rockets and torpedoes but no sign of a nuclear weapon.

In April 1945, the American military arrested Hahn in Tailfingen. He, Heisenberg, and eight others were moved to a country estate near Cambridge, England, called Farm Hall. The scientists were in shock when Germany surrendered on May 7. Hitler had lost the war? He had killed himself in an underground bunker? It was incomprehensible.

The scientists complained about their terrible treatment while also reminding one another not to let people know how comfortable the conditions actually were. They didn't know it, but everything they said was recorded on secret microphones hidden throughout the manor house. On their first day in the house, this conversation was captured:

KURT DIEBNER: I wonder whether there are microphones installed here?

WERNER HEISENBERG: Microphones installed? (laughing) Oh no, they're not as cute as all that. I don't think they know the real Gestapo methods; they're a bit old fashioned in that respect.

Operation Epsilon, the detention of these scientists, was meant to learn precisely the extent of their knowledge of nuclear fission and bomb building. What it revealed was that the scientists, as brilliant as they considered themselves to be, had no idea that an atomic weapon could actually be built.

Not only could it be built–it already had been. At the end of May 1945, a meeting was held in Washington, D.C., to discuss the atomic bomb. Germany may have surrendered, but the fight in the Pacific against Japan ground on. The Japanese were thought too stubborn, too devoted to the emperor, to ever surrender.

The first atomic test was scheduled for July, near Los Alamos in the Alamogordo desert. Scientists suggested that the Soviets be invited to witness the powerful weapon, so that all could agree to avoid a future nuclear arms race. They wrote a letter to the president, pleading that the bomb not be used as a weapon of war, only as a deterrent. The military held a different view: They wanted the bomb to be used on Japan, as clear, convincing proof of American military superiority. As a follow-up, the United States would halt production on any more bombs as proof of good faith and moral intentions.

In an argument between scientists and generals, it's easy to guess who won. Bohr had been worried about precisely this use of the bomb. He thought it should be used only to deter destruction, not cause it. And the possibility of an arms race, of several countries developing their own superbombs, scared him even more.

Bohr was focused on the bomb, but Meitner had forgotten about it as soon as Germany surrendered. What need for a bomb with Hitler dead and the Reich collapsed? Meitner had her own fears and worries. She was horrified by the news of death camps, all so much worse than the rumors. These weren't prisoner camps but places of mass murder. Millions of people had been exterminated, six million of them Jewish men, women, and children. Stockholm housed some of the refugees freed from the camps, and seeing their shaved heads and emaciated bodies filled Meitner with an agonizing bleakness. Germany had done this, her Germany. This was the country that had given her so much, the place she had thought the most educated and civilized in the world. More than that, her own friends and colleagues had been complicit in this enormous crime against humanity. They had looked the other way, they had rationalized, they had allowed it all to happen.

Meitner hadn't confronted Hahn when he'd worked on toxic gas during World War I. She hadn't criticized him when he received the Emil Fischer Medal while she was awarded only a copy. She hadn't argued with him when he'd taken full credit for her discovery of nuclear fission. But this was something she couldn't ignore. For once, she wasn't timid or solicitous. She was furious. She wrote to him:

> *Dear Otto,*
> *This month, I have written a great number of letters to you in my mind, because it was clear to me that even people like you and Laue have not grasped the real situation. I noticed this so clearly among other things when Laue wrote to me on the occasion of* [the biologist Fritz von] *Wettstein's death, that his death was a loss also in the wider sense, because of his diplomatic talents. W. could have been very useful at the end of the war. How could a man who had never objected to the crimes of recent years be of use to Germany? Precisely that has been Germany's misfortune: that all of you lost your standards of justice and fairness. As early as March, 1935, you told me that* [the chemist Philipp Heinrich] *Hörlein had told you that horrible things would be done to the Jews. He knew about all the crimes that had been planned and that later would be carried out; in spite of that he was a member of the* [Nazi] *party and you still regarded him—in spite of it—as a very respectable man, and let him guide you in your behavior toward your best friend* [referring to herself].

All of you also worked for Nazi Germany, and never attempted passive resistance. Of course, to save your troubled consciences you occasionally helped an oppressed person; still you let millions of innocent people be murdered, and there was never a sound of protest.

I must write you this because so much of what happens to you and Germany now depends upon your recognizing what all of you allowed to happen . . . I believe, as do many others, that one possibility would be for you to make a statement, namely that you know you bear a responsibility for the occurrences as a result of your passivity, and that you feel it necessary to help make reparations—as far as the past can be made good . . .

This sounds merciless, and yet, believe me, it is out of the truest friendship that I write all this to you. You really can't expect the world to pity Germany. What we have heard recently about the unfathomable atrocities of the concentration camps exceeds everything we had feared. When I heard a very objective report about Belsen and Buchenwald on the British radio, I began to cry out loud and could not sleep all night. And if you had seen the people who came here from the camps . . . They should force a man like Heisenberg, and millions of others with him, to see these camps and tortured people. His performance in Denmark in 1941 cannot be forgotten. [She is referring to the famous conversation with Bohr, fishing for information about atomic weapons, while posing as morally superior.]

You might remember while I was still in Germany (and today I know that it was not only stupid but very unfair of me not to have gone away immediately) I often said to you, "As long as just we [the Jews] *and not you have sleepless nights, it won't get any better in Germany." But you never had even one sleepless night. You didn't want to see it; it was too inconvenient. I could prove it to you with many examples, big and small. Please believe me that all I write here is an attempt to help you all.*

With very affectionate greetings to everyone. Yours,

Meitner

Meitner knew Hahn well. He was doing exactly what she expected—asking the world to pity Germany. The microphones at Farm Hall recorded him insisting on what a moral person he'd been, Meitner herself being proof: ". . . in 1938 when the non-Aryan Fraulein Meitner was still there—it wasn't easy to keep her in my Institute." He conveniently forgot how he had pushed her to leave, kicking her out himself.

Hahn wasn't alone in this self-serving attitude. All of the scientists complained about their treatment–held prisoner in comfortable furnishings, with ample food and pleasant grounds to walk in. Weizsäcker even hoped to stay long-term. Asked about him, Erich Bagge replied, "He says every day that he has never had such a good opportunity to think and work as he has here."

The scientists considered the Americans absolute brutes in their treatment of Germany. Germany was the real victim. In all the recorded conversations, German atrocities were rarely mentioned and then usually in the context of excusing themselves from any responsibility: "If Hitler ordered a few atrocities in concentration camps during the last few years, one can always say that these occurred under the stress of war but now we have peace and Germany has surrendered unconditionally and they can't do the same things to us now."

Karl Wirtz, a physicist on Heisenberg's team, was alone in admitting, "We have done things which are unique in the world. We went to Poland and not only murdered the Jews in Poland, but for instance, the SS drove up to a girls' school, fetched out the top class and shot them simply because the girls were High School girls and the intelligentsia were to be wiped out. Just imagine if they arrived in Hechingen [a small German town], drove up to the girls' school and shot all the girls! That's what we did."

There was no response to this from any of the scientists. The conversation was over.

Mostly, they strategized about how they could appear valuable to their captors and worried about what would happen to them after the war was finally over. Erich Bagge suggested, "We must tell the Americans that Heisenberg is the only man in the world who is able to make the bomb."

Meitner sent the letter to Hahn but didn't hear back. She didn't know that Hahn had been arrested and hadn't received it. When she confronted him about it later, he insisted he didn't know what she was talking about. She thought he was erasing her once again, noting on her copy of the letter: "A letter that did not reach him" in disbelieving quotation marks.

THIRTY-FIVE

THE MOTHER OF THE BOMB

That summer of 1945, Meitner stayed at a friend's cottage in Leksand, along a Swedish lake. She was there when the first atomic bomb was dropped on Hiroshima, Japan.
Her friend rushed to tell her.
I have terrible news . . .
WHAT!!!
Meitner burst into tears. Had her "beautiful discovery" caused this? She'd only wanted the truth. Not this massive destruction.
Miss Meitner? I'm from the *Leksand Daily*. We'd love to interview the mother of the bomb.
Mother of the bomb?! NEVER!!!
August 7, 1945: Reporters from all over called Meitner, eager to hear what the "Jewish mother of the bomb" had to say. The blast was so powerful, it was the equivalent of 20,000 *tons* of TNT, *plus* the toxic effects of radiation poisoning. Meitner was horrified.

Meitner refused to talk to reporters, but that didn't stop them from inventing interviews with her. One headline, "Fleeing Jewess," claimed she had escaped Hitler with the secret of the bomb and rushed to give it to the Allies. Another called her "The Lady with the Bomb in Her Purse," as if she had escaped with a bomb recipe tucked in her handbag. She was often described as the "Jewish mother of the bomb." The *New York Times* featured a series of ridiculous headlines, none of them true: "Reich Exile Emerges as Heroine in Denial to Nazis of Atom's Secret"—forgetting that this "secret" had been published in *Nature.* Another blared, "Dr. Meitner Says Hitler Tried to Force Her to Stay in Reich to Continue Atom Research"—when the Nazis had kicked her out of any kind of research work. The stories described her as a "brilliant mathematician," rather than a physicist. But they got one quote from her right: "I must stress that I myself have not in any way worked on the smashing of the atom with the idea of producing death-dealing weapons. You must not blame us scientists for the use to which war technicians have put our discoveries."

Meitner, who had always been cringingly shy, was suddenly thrust into the spotlight. Everyone wanted to talk to her, write about her, meet her. She was getting the respect she'd always craved, but not for what she wanted and definitely not in the way she wanted.

The first major radio interview she agreed to was with Eleanor Roosevelt–she could hardly say no to the widow of the American president (who had died in April). Roosevelt began by recognizing Meitner's major contribution to science:

> When I read the dramatic story of the way in which this new discovery had been started, and that a woman had played such an important part in it, it gave me a feeling of great responsibility. It is a tremendous force, and if a woman was given the opportunity to discover it, certainly other women throughout the world have an obligation to see that it is used now to bring the war to a close, and to save human lives, and that in the future, it is used for the good of all mankind, and not for destructive purposes. I wonder if I might ask Dr. Meitner what her feeling was when she first heard of the dropping of the bomb, and realized that it might bring this destructive war to a close.

Meitner answered, "I agree—perfectly—that women have a responsibility—and we are obliged to try—so far as we can—to prevent another war. And I hope the construction of the atom bomb not only will help to finish this awful war, these wars here and in Japan, but that we will be able to use this large energy release for peaceful work."

Roosevelt went on to compare Meitner to the most famous woman scientist everyone knew—Marie Curie—calling both of them a symbol for women of the future. Meitner used her time on the radio to call for more women to work in the sciences and in the peace process. She urged that atomic energy should be used only for "peaceful work." After Roosevelt signed off, the interview continued in a more informal way with the Swedish host. He asked Meitner about her work and ended with a question about what she thought nuclear fission could be used for in times of peace. Meitner's reply was an accurate prediction: "It could be used to drive submarines, aircraft, and industrial power."

In the radio interview, Meitner was calm and composed. In her letters to friends, she revealed her shock at what nuclear fission had led to: "What I do know now! What I did foresee long ago! And what indeed has become inconceivable reality."

THIRTY-SIX

THE AMERICANS DID WHAT?!

At Farm Hall, the German physicists were stunned by the news of the bomb. Heisenberg insisted it had to be a hoax—the atomic bomb was simply impossible.

All I can suggest is that some dilettante in America who knows very little about it has bluffed them in saying 'If you drop this it has the equivalent of 20,000 tons of high explosive' and in reality doesn't work at all. I am willing to believe that it is a high pressure bomb and I don't believe that it has anything to do with uranium."
I think it's dreadful of the Americans to have done it. I think it is madness on their part.
One can't say that. One could equally well say 'That's the quickest way to end the war.' Well, how have they actually done it? I find it a disgrace if we, the Professors who have worked on it, cannot at least work out how they did it.

Heisenberg consoled himself with this explanation: "The point is that the whole structure of the relationship between the scientist and the state in Germany was such that although we were not 100% anxious to do it, on the other hand we were so little trusted by the state that even if we had wanted to do it, it would not have been easy to get it through."

It wasn't the professors' fault then, but the Reich's.

Once they got over the shock of the bomb's reality, the German scientists congratulated themselves that they hadn't done such work. They told themselves that it wasn't a question of their capability but of their moral superiority. The Third Reich would never have used such a terrible weapon. Only the Americans were capable of such brutish, cowardly behavior. As Carl Friedrich von Weizsäcker said:

> History will record that the Americans and the English made a bomb, and that at the same time the Germans, under the Hitler regime, produced a workable engine. In other words, the peaceful development of a uranium engine was made in Germany under the Hitler regime, whereas the Americans and the English developed this ghastly weapon of war.

In fact, even the "workable" engine hadn't been finished, though the Nazis could honestly claim its "development."

Hitler, in this comparison, was clearly the good guy. Never mind that Speer wrote in his memoir that Hitler would happily have used an atomic weapon, if only his scientists had been capable of building one. Heisenberg himself admitted as much.

Three days after Hiroshima, a second bomb was detonated over Nagasaki, Japan. Again, the German scientists flailed, trying to understand how two such complicated devices could have been made. Again, Meitner was interviewed on international radio.

This time, the notes taken by the British officers at Farm Hall included a description of Hahn's reaction: "He has been very shattered by the announcement of the use of the atomic bomb as he feels responsible for the lives of so many people in view of his original discovery. He has taken the fact that Professor Meitner has been credited by the press with the original discovery very well although he points out that she was in fact one of his assistants and had already left Berlin at the time of his discovery."

Even as a political prisoner with his country in ruins, Hahn's first concern was that Meitner was getting accolades he felt he alone deserved. He was desperate for the world to know of his incredible work.

The whole of Heisenberg's Uranium Group was so angry

that the credit for the impressive new bomb had been taken from them, they wrote a letter, dated August 8, 1945, spelling out how much of the groundbreaking work had been done by themselves in Germany. They gave Meitner and Frisch barely an acknowledgment: "The Hahn discovery was checked in many laboratories, particularly in the United States, shortly after publication. Various research workers, Meitner and Frisch were probably the first, pointed out the enormous energies which were released by the fission of uranium. On the other hand, Meitner had left Berlin six months before the discovery and was not concerned herself in the discovery."

The letter omitted mentioning that the "discovery" wasn't replicated in "many laboratories" until Meitner's interpretation was reported by Bohr at the physics conference. Hahn's initial article described a failure, not a discovery. It's also notable that Meitner and Frisch were downgraded to "research workers," that they weren't credited with discovering fission, only with noticing the energy released by splitting the uranium atom. Hahn and his colleagues were rewriting history right away, trying to affirm his pivotal role and erase Meitner's. Even as the letter asserting Hahn's importance was written, Heisenberg admitted, "I still do not understand what they have done."

The public was hearing about Meitner for the first time,

but the physics community already knew her reputation. And they knew it was her interpretation that had given meaning to Hahn's experiments. Karl Herzfeld, another Jewish Austrian physicist working in the United States, invited Meitner to lecture at the Catholic University of America in Washington, D.C., then stay as a visiting professor for that winter.

Meitner, who had hesitated so many times before about going anywhere in the English-speaking world, accepted. She would see her nephew, her sisters who were in New York, her many colleagues who had found new positions in America. Before she left, Meitner's new fame earned her election to the Royal Swedish Academy of Sciences, a recognition given to only two other women before her: Eva Ekeblad in 1748 and Marie Curie in 1910. At last, her adopted home was honoring her, though not with the Nobel Prize she'd been nominated for so many times.

Meitner was finally being valued for all the hard work and sharp insights she'd had over the years. At last, she was getting the credit she deserved for nuclear fission. She just wished it hadn't taken a bomb for that to happen.

THIRTY-SEVEN

MEITNER IN AMERICA

Life need not be easy. provided that it is not empty.

An American lecture tour was arranged. Meitner would start at Catholic University and continue to Harvard, Princeton, the Massachusetts Institute of Technology (MIT), Brown, Sweet Briar, and Wellesley. Arriving in the United States, she was welcomed by Einstein, Fermi, Bohr, Szilard, and Frisch.

Meitner refused to talk to reporters, but huge crowds came to hear her. She spoke about the need for more women in science and academia, about the importance of searching for the truth. The shy woman who had fought so hard for an education was given honorary degrees at Ivy League colleges.

In February 1946, she was guest of honor at the Women's National Press Club's awards ceremony. She was seated next to President Harry Truman.

Ah, so you're the little lady who got us into this mess!
Um . . . well . . .

Meitner had never supported making the bomb. All she could do now was try to ensure that an atomic weapon would never be used again.

At a cocktail party for Catholic University officials given in her honor, Meitner met Major General Leslie Groves, the man in charge of the Manhattan Project. Meitner had absolutely no idea what to say to him. He was proud of his incredible accomplishment, the vast logistics of so many people working on such complicated problems, all coming together with great organizational skill. She wrote down their brief conversation in her diary:

> Groves told me that when he saw the first [atomic] pile in Chicago, he understood everything in half an hour, and was able to give 6 or 7 good suggestions . . . Bohr was of no help at all.
>
> I: Nevertheless, he is the greatest living physicist.
>
> He: All theoretical physicists are prima donnas.

Groves was proud of what he'd done–it was an impressive organizational accomplishment–though Bohr undeniably played an important role. Meitner was sorry so much effort had been put into so destructive a device. When she brought up the issue, "I felt that the manner in which he spoke of the work on the bomb was intended to cut off any questions from me."

Universities weren't the only places clamoring for Meitner—Hollywood wanted to make a movie about her. MGM loved the dramatic story of her escape from Germany. The movie would be called *The Beginning of the End*. Meitner, disgusted by the "escaping with a bomb in the purse" plot taken from tabloid headlines, said she'd rather walk naked down Broadway. She refused to have anything to do with the project. The producers turned instead to her nephew Frisch, who was happy to play the role of scientific adviser. He didn't expect the movie to be accurate (it wasn't), but it was entertaining and paid him a nice bonus. His one complaint was that all the scientist characters were American, when in reality, the scientists were German, Austrian, Hungarian, Italian, Polish, Russian, Danish, and mostly Jewish, with very few Americans. Robert Oppenheimer, the physicist in charge, was one of the few Americans involved. Ernest Lawrence was another. It was a vast immigrant project.

After a semester of teaching, many lectures, and a host of honors, Meitner returned to Stockholm. The war was over now. She could go back to Berlin. But what was waiting for her there? And how could she work on physics with the weight of what her discovery had caused?

THIRTY-EIGHT

THE NOBEL PRIZE FOR NUCLEAR FISSION GOES TO . . .

November 1945: The Nobel Prize in Chemistry for 1944 was awarded a year late, under committee rules. The award went to Hahn for discovering nuclear fission. Meitner had been nominated, but Hahn alone was recognized.

Hahn was still at Farm Hall when he got the news. He was pleased—then outraged.

I am a Nobel Prize winner! How can you keep me prisoner here?!
THIS IS MONSTROUS!!

Major T. H. Rittner, in charge of Farm Hall, described the scene: "Hahn came to see me in the afternoon, having obviously worked himself up into a state of courageous fury. He was red in the face and was shaking all over even when he first came into the room. He said . . . our guests here are treated worse than war criminals in that they had no proper communication with their families and are detained without even a charge being brought against them. I tried to say that I had no objections to his writing such a letter, but that I did not think that the chances of it being delivered were particularly bright. Hahn, however, was hardly in a mood to consider my replies and left the room abruptly."

The conditions that Hahn found so atrocious were described by a fellow scientist, Karl Wirtz, at the end of their six months at Farm Hall: "It would be a mistake, when we get back to Germany, to say how *marvellous* everything has been."

"Yes," agreed Heisenberg. "That should be avoided at all costs, but, on the other hand, we must do justice to the British who really have treated us extremely well."

Once he heard that he could go to Stockholm to receive the Nobel Prize, Hahn calmed down. He still felt badly treated, but the award was a big consolation, proof of his high status in the world of science.

The Nobel Prize committee didn't represent the physics community, however. Anyone working on nuclear physics knew the truth and was surprised that the committee had blatantly ignored Fritz Strassmann, who had done the work alongside Hahn, and Meitner and Frisch, who had interpreted and given meaning to the experiments. Without the physicists, there would have been no discovery of nuclear fission, just some odd-looking experiments that Hahn presented as failures. After the atomic bombs were dropped on Nagasaki and Hiroshima, the whole world knew Meitner's role in the discovery. Some scientists joked that Lise Meitner's crowning achievement was a Nobel Prize for Otto Hahn. But the lapse was quickly swept under the rug. Nobody spoke out in Meitner's favor, just as they hadn't when Jews were kicked out of jobs in Germany. For Meitner, it was an all-too-familiar feeling.

Hahn called Meitner a "bitter, disappointed woman," his usual criticism of her. When she complained about how Jews were treated, she was "bitter." When she chafed at being described as his assistant rather than partner, she was "bitter." And when she accused him of kicking her out of the KWI, she was "bitter."

In December 1945, at the Nobel Prize ceremony, Hahn gave Strassman some credit, even mentioning Meitner and Frisch. But in the lecture after the ceremony, he presented the discovery as his alone.

Meitner expected that even though the prize had been awarded only to Hahn, he would set the record straight and tell the world about her essential role. She sat waiting, her face hardening, as he talked about his amazing research. There was not one word about her revolutionary interpretation of the experiments Hahn had found so puzzling.

Photographs captured Meitner and Hahn together at the

Nobel event, looking awkward, not at all like longtime friends and partners. Meitner couldn't say what she wanted, and Hahn had no interest in asking. This was his moment to shine, and he wouldn't let anything ruin that. He didn't want to be reminded of Nazi crimes or of any earlier connection to Meitner. She should, he thought, be happy for him.

Meitner wrote in a letter that Hahn was "forgetting the past and instead stressing the injustice that is being done to Germany. Since I am a part of the past to be repressed, Hahn has not mentioned our long cooperation or even my name in those interviews in which he talked about his life's work."

Hahn described the same evening: "I had quite an unhappy conversation with Lise Meitner, who said I should not have sent her out of Germany when I did. The discord probably stemmed from a certain disappointment that I alone was awarded the [Nobel] prize. I did not talk to Lise Meitner about that, however, but a number of her friends alluded to it in a rather unfriendly manner. But I was really not at fault; I had only been looking after the welfare of my respected colleague when I prepared her emigration. And after all, the prize was awarded to me just for work I did alone or with my colleague Fritz Strassmann."

Hahn's memory conveniently omitted that he didn't help her leave the country—Coster and Debye did. Nor did he do any kind of preparations beyond hosting her for her last night in Berlin and offering her his mother's ring. Clearly, he knew that he owed a lot to Meitner, that he never would have understood fission as happening, because he gave a large share of the prize money to her. He may not have been willing to share the public fame, but his conscience urged him to at least split the money.

Meitner, disgusted with such a feeble gesture, gave every penny to the Emergency Committee of Atomic Scientists, in Princeton, helping to settle Jewish refugee scientists. Hahn may have forgotten her refugee status, but she hadn't.

THIRTY-NINE

AFTER THE WAR: WORKING FOR NUCLEAR PEACE

The KWI was renamed the Max Planck Institute for Physics. Hahn and Strassmann helped with the "denazification" process by clearing all the scientists they wanted to work with, fervent Nazis included.

Meitner was appalled. She'd hoped for some recognition of the wrongs Nazi Germany had done, some admission from her colleagues that their silence had been a form of complicity, that they had allowed Jews to be kicked out—and murdered.

Hahn refused any moral responsibility, seeing himself as the real victim. This hurt Meitner even more than the Nobel Prize snub. She wrote to friends about her fear and despair.

He [Hahn] suppresses the Nazi crimes.
I find it quite painful that in his interviews [Hahn] did not say one word about me, to say nothing of our thirty years of work together.
His motivation is somewhat complicated. He is convinced that Germans are being treated unjustly, the more so in that he simply suppresses the past. As for me, I am part of the suppressed past.
In a letter to me he wrote, for instance, that the Americans in Germany are now doing the same as the Germans used to do in the occupied countries. I answered him, that he could not have meant that seriously . . . He cannot disregard the fact that the Germans killed millions of innocent people. He did not respond to this and when he was here, he asked me not to talk about politics . . .

Hahn staked the moral high ground by insisting that German scientists had developed the atomic bomb before the Americans had, but they chose not to let loose such an evil on humanity. The Nazis weren't guilty of genocide—the Americans were, in the bombing of Nagasaki and Hiroshima. The fact that Heisenberg's group hadn't thought it was possible to build a nuclear weapon didn't trouble Hahn.

Meitner wrote, "Hahn himself surely did not want to work on a bomb, but in one interview he made the statement, 'He was glad the Germans were not burdened with the responsibility for the bomb and the resulting meaningless deaths of thousands of people in Hiroshima' . . . What he ought to have said was that he was glad about it because Germany had done so many other things that were much worse, but he was unable to say that." Hahn had conveniently forgotten his own—and Germany's—work on poison gas during World War I. He felt absolutely no responsibility for the deaths caused then. For Meitner, it was all part of the same willful blindness.

In 1947, Hahn wrote to Meitner, offering her the position

of head of the physics department at her old institute, now the Max Planck Institute. How many women were heads of any department? None! Hahn felt he was being magnanimous, allowing such an unprecedented appointment. Meitner declined, saying that as a Jew and an Austrian, she wouldn't feel comfortable. She wrote, "The Germans have still not understood what has happened and have forgotten all horrors which they did not experience personally. I think I would not be able to breathe in this atmosphere." As for the friendship Hahn thought he was offering, Meitner already mourned its loss. "It is clear to me that Hahn was hardly aware of his lack of friendship, and he wrote to me . . . thanking me completely naively for my 'great friendship' . . . Perhaps our generation is too old to see things clearly and no longer has the strength to battle the prevailing spiritual disorders that go back more than a hundred years and happened to find an especially gruesome expression in nazism."

The statement of responsibility and deep regret that Meitner had hoped Hahn would make, that she wished the German scientific community would make, never happened. Hahn wrote her, "One cannot do anything to counteract a terror regime . . . How can one constantly reproach an entire people for their behavior during such times? . . . We all know that

Hitler was responsible for the war and the unspeakable misery all over the world, but there must be some sort of world understanding also for the German people."

Laue, despite having stood up to the Nazis, went further, writing an article protesting that most German scientists had never worked for the Reich. Meitner complained to Hahn about the essay:

> Is it really justifiable to say that the majority of scientists were against Hitler from the beginning? . . . When Planck held the obsequies for Haber, Laue and [Wolfgang] Heubner were the only professors to dare to come to it. At the same time the Chemical Society and the Glass Engineering Society . . . had forbidden their members from attending . . . Doesn't this all show that the subordination to the Hitler ideas was very prevalent and that the opposition . . . was a minority? I truly do not have the intention of saying unpleasant things with these observations, but I am afraid that with his inclination to defend everything that has happened—out of an understandable attachment to Germany—Laue is not helping Germany, but risks achieving the opposite . . .

She wrote to Laue about turning down the position Hahn offered, "in part because I am Austrian, and in part because of my Jewish origins." As she later commented, "Laue wrote that it was a pity, as they had no objections to Austrians."

Meitner was deeply disturbed by this strain in her former friends, this entrenched unwillingness to admit passive complicity, along with absolutely no recognition of the poisonous anti-Semitism still embedded in German culture. It was a chasm they would never bridge. Meitner would never return to Germany to live. As she wrote to Hahn: "Those who remained in Germany during the war will say 'She didn't really EARN her place here.'" She stayed in Stockholm, wondering where to go next and what to do.

While Hahn focused on rebuilding German science and reestablishing his career, Meitner turned her attention to science's ethical responsibilities. She spoke about scientists' need for a moral framework, the dangers of creating Frankenstein monsters in the name of progress. She may have sparked the work on the atomic bomb, but she was determined that physics should return to the pure search for truth she'd always loved.

FORTY

A PRIZE OF HER OWN

In 1949, Meitner won the Max Planck Medal, along with Hahn. The two longtime partners were finally recognized as equals. For the first time since fleeing in 1938, Meitner returned to Berlin. She was greeted like a returning hero, celebrated at dinners and taken on a tour of the city.

In many ways, it was a very different place. But she was dismayed by what hadn't changed. The ugly anti-Semitism remained. The supposed "denazification" process meant nothing as zealous Nazis were protected, remaining in powerful positions.

Now that Germany was acclaiming her at last, she should have felt joyful. Instead, she was depressed. Hahn's refusal to discuss the Nobel Prize and the war chilled her deeply. Meitner clearly didn't belong in *Germany*—and didn't want to belong.

We're rebuilding! You can be part of the new Germany!
I fear it's the same old Germany.
ACHTUNG! IN 70 METERS YOU ENTER EAST BERLIN

Meitner never did get her frozen pension from the KWI. There was no recognition of any losses she may have suffered. The new *Germany*—and its scientists—wanted to focus on the future, not be dragged down by the past.

As the "Grand Lady of Nuclear Physics," Meitner had her own lab in Stockholm and worked with Dr. Sigvard Eklund, who would later be the director general of the International Atomic Energy Agency. She was determined to prove that atomic energy could be useful, peaceful, a gift to humanity rather than a curse. With Eklund, she built the first experimental reactor in Sweden, a step toward making a power-generating nuclear reactor. It took more than a decade, but she won the respect of her Swedish colleagues, though as usual, she felt on the edge of things. Wherever she went, she was always the only woman in the room, and the feeling of not quite belonging never left her.

Science remained her life, though, and she worked until 1954, retiring at age seventy-five. The previous year, she wrote to Hahn about the revisionist history she saw firmly rooted in Germany. She hadn't given up on changing his mind and hoped that he could be wiser now that he was older. She described how all her achievements had been erased. German literature mentioned her only as a "long-term co-worker of Hahn." She asked him, "What would you say if you were to be characterized as a 'long-term co-worker' of mine? After the last fifteen years, which I wouldn't wish on a good friend, shall my scientific past also be taken from me? Is that fair? And why is it happening?"

He said nothing.

Meitner had published 128 books and articles. She had made major discoveries, including the one that defined the twentieth century. She was nominated for the Nobel Prize in Chemistry or Physics forty-eight times: twenty-nine for physics, nineteen for chemistry. Yet Hahn never acknowledged Meitner's role in the prize that should have been hers as well. In articles about Hahn and nuclear fission, there was little mention of Meitner beyond the phrase she hated so much, "long-term co-worker." The reconciliation Meitner fervently hoped for never came.

Then, in 1955, Meitner was awarded the newly minted Otto Hahn Prize for Chemistry and Physics, given by the German Chemical Society. At the ceremony, Hahn presented the medal to her with a wink, saying, "Now, dear Lise, I may give the name to this award, but you get the money. Now you can buy me a beer!" Meitner's stiff grin in the award photo shows exactly what she thought of that offer.

Even after she left her position, Meitner never gave up physics. Instead, she focused on political questions concerning science, including the status of women in science and the military use of nuclear energy. She worked at the United Nations' International Atomic Energy Agency on control of nuclear weapons until her mid-eighties, hoping to leave the world a safer place.

Meitner died in 1968, shortly before her ninetieth birthday. She didn't know it, but Hahn had died several months earlier, their ends twined together as their lives had been.

Her epitaph reads: "A physicist who never lost her humanity."

Meitner's nuclear fission experimental setup, 1938, reconstructed at the Deutsches Museum, Munich. It is still credited by some as the work of "the team of Otto Hahn and Fritz Strassmann," giving no mention of Lise Meitner.

AFTERWORD

Decades after her death, the woman who had been so famous was erased from the history of physics yet again. All the credit for discovering nuclear fission was given to Otto Hahn alone. Recent articles about Hahn, including his Wikipedia page, discount Meitner's revolutionary interpretation of his experiments. The German Museum in Munich featured a replica of Meitner's famous worktable from her basement lab with the apparatus she had built. But the descriptive plaque commemorated the equipment as what Hahn had used for his Nobel Prize–winning discovery, with no mention of Meitner. The audiotape that accompanied the display is in Hahn's voice, with not a word about Meitner. In the fall of 1989, Berlin and Munich developed a traveling exhibit on the history of atomic power, including the worktable. Fifty years after her revolutionary discovery, the German science community finally mentioned Meitner's role in the exhibit, but her name was kept off the permanent display in 1990 for "financial reasons." The plaque listing honored scientists at the Austrian Institute for Radium Research and Nuclear Physics (now the Stefan Meyer Institute for Subatomic Physics) still doesn't include Meitner. Other names—Henri Becquerel, Norman F. Ramsey, Curie—are there, but not Vienna's own citizen.

Two years later, in 1992, a group of scientists from the Society for Heavy Ion Research in Darmstadt, Germany, again tried to make up for this lapse in the history of science. They proposed naming element 109, one of the heaviest known elements, after Meitner. In 1994, the International Union of Pure and Applied Chemistry, the commission in charge of naming elements, approved element 109 as meitnerium, or Mt. Meitnerium is now part of the periodic table, along with

Meitner (*lower right corner*), the only woman physicist in the room, attends a conference of physicists at the Niels Bohr Institute, Copenhagen, 1937. (The other woman in the room was not a physicist.)

other elements named after famous scientists, such as rutherfordium, seaborgium, bohrium, roentgenium, copernicium, mendelevium, nobelium, lawrencium, fermium, einsteinium, and curium. Meitner, nominated almost fifty times for a Nobel Prize, had finally joined the list of the most important physicists, a place where she has long belonged. She would be happy to know she's still part of physics, that beautiful science, and its search for truth.

Lise Meitner, twenty-one years old, in winter garden, Vienna, 1899

AUTHOR'S NOTE

I was introduced to Lise Meitner by my son, a physics major who had learned about her in a college class. He knew my interest in women who should be better known but are lost to history simply because they were women. But he warned me of the difficulty of the subject. Meitner's discovery was pivotal in the twentieth century but had become synonymous with horrific destruction. Her achievement would be morally tricky to write about even though she refused to work on developing a bomb based on her science. I turned to a physicist friend, Warren Heckrotte, who had spent a lifetime negotiating nuclear arms reductions with the Soviets. He thought Meitner would bear up to close ethical scrutiny. She had never meant her findings to be used as a weapon of war and had worked for nuclear peace herself. He handed me the first of the books I would read in my lengthy research.

As I read more, I found Meitner difficult on an unexpected level. Her stubborn refusal to leave Berlin, long after all her Jewish friends and colleagues had fled the country, looked foolish to our contemporary eyes. We, of course, know about what happened to the German Jews, the brutality of the Holocaust, Hitler's "Final Solution" to rid the world of Jews.

Meitner and Hahn sit at their first worktable, Berliner University, 1909

But Meitner could not have imagined that civilized Germany would ever organize such racial mass murder. What helped me as I read about her paralysis and as I wrote about it myself was a set of family letters. These are letters written to my father-in-law in the United States from his family left behind in Chodorov, a town in Galicia (now Khodoriv, Ukraine). The letters date from 1935 to 1940, starting with minor descriptions of things getting harder for Jews, ending with desperate pleas for help getting them the paperwork and money they needed to leave the country. Like most Jews, they didn't realize how dire the situation was until it was too late. The last letter doesn't hint at their fate, but they were then in Lwów, Poland (now Lviv, Ukraine) hoping for help from the American consulate. Instead, they were massacred, along with the other Jewish residents of the city.

Reading the letters again put Meitner's apparent blinders into perspective. Yes, she should have left sooner, but she, like millions of others, like my in-laws, couldn't imagine the death camps. The family letters gave me a new light to understand Meitner's apparent foolishness. She had faith in humanity, in people. That should be a strength, not a weakness. That

Meitner and Hahn work on radioactivity in their lab at the Kaiser Wilhelm Institute of Chemistry, Berlin-Dahlem, 1913.

the times proved her wrong isn't a mark against her. It's a warning to all of us not to be complacent.

By focusing on Meitner's work, as she did herself, I found the story that needed to be told: how a brilliant woman was marginalized first because of her gender, then because of her ethnicity, and ultimately by her gender again when the Nobel Prize went to a man who had no concept at all of nuclear fission, rather than to the woman who had described exactly what happened. This book is my attempt to set the record straight, to give Meitner the place in history, in our memories, that she deserves to have.

Meitner, on the steps of the chemistry building at Bryn Mawr, talks to young scientists Sue Jones Swisher, Rosalie Hoyt, and Danna Pearson McDonough, students at the all-women's college, 1959.

TIMELINE OF MEITNER'S LIFE AND ACHIEVEMENTS

NOVEMBER 7, 1878: Lise Meitner is born in Vienna, Austria, the third child of Philipp and Hedwig Meitner.

1892: Meitner finishes school at the all-girls' Bürgerschule in Vienna.

1899: Women are allowed in Austrian colleges to study science and medicine. Meitner starts studying for the Matura, the Viennese high school exit exam.

1901: Meitner enrolls as the first woman at the University of Vienna in physics.

1906: Meitner finishes her dissertation and is the second woman at the University of Vienna to earn a PhD in physics.

1907: Meitner moves to Berlin. Starts working with Otto Hahn on beta decay of radioactive substances.

Meitner publishes two articles, "On the Dispersion of Alpha Rays" by herself and "On the Absorption of the Beta Rays of Several Radioelements" with Hahn, both in *Physikalische Zeitschrift*.

Meitner and Hahn discover a short-lived radioactive element, "actinium C."

Meitner develops the "recoil method," a widely used way to physically separate elements in order to study particles that are emitted.

1908: The law changes in Germany to allow women to receive college degrees.

1912: Max Planck hires Meitner as his paid assistant at the University of Berlin.

JUNE 28, 1914: Archduke Franz Ferdinand, heir presumptive to the Austro-Hungarian throne, is assassinated in Sarajevo, provoking Austria to invade Serbia. Austria's ally, Germany, quickly declares war on Russia, Serbia's ally, with Russian allies France and Britain soon taking part, too. The Great War begins (later known as World War I).

The Kaiser Wilhelm Institute (KWI) promotes Meitner from "guest" physicist to a full-time paid position.

1915: Meitner works as a volunteer X-ray nurse/technician for the Austrian army near the Russian front.

1917: Meitner returns from military duty. She sets up the physics department at the KWI.

1918: Meitner and Hahn publish their paper about discovering protactinium.

Albert Einstein and Meitner discuss doing research on gamma radiation together but abandon the project when they see that others have already written on the same topic.

Meitner and Hahn publish eight articles during World War I.

Meitner is made head of the radiophysics department at the KWI.

NOVEMBER 11, 1918: Armistice Day, end of World War I.

1919: Meitner is given a long-term contract at the KWI and a raise in salary.

1920: The KWI creates separate departments for physics and chemistry. Meitner and Hahn continue their joint research.

1921: Meitner visits Niels Bohr's Institute for Theoretical Physics in Copenhagen, the start of a long, close friendship.

JULY 29, 1921: Adolf Hitler is elected chairman of the National Socialist German Workers' Party (commonly called the Nazi party).

1922: Meitner publishes six papers on nuclear models, gamma rays, and beta rays.

Meitner becomes one of the first women in Germany named assistant professor, with full salary and benefits.

1923: Meitner publishes two papers on what was later called the "Auger effect," bringing her total of published articles to fifty-eight.

Nazi groups start to organize more widely in Germany and Austria. In Munich, Hitler leads a failed coup against the government ("the Beer Hall Putsch").

Due to inflation following steep reparations paid to France and Britain after World War I, the German mark totally collapses in value, worth almost nothing.

1924: Meitner and Hahn are nominated for the Nobel Prize in Chemistry.

Meitner is nominated for the Leibniz Prize by the Berlin Academy of Sciences and wins the Silver Medal, the first time the prize goes to a woman.

Meitner coauthors the *Yearbook for the Institute for Chemistry*.

Meitner is the first scientist to publish experiments using a cloud chamber, a device she built herself.

Hitler is sentenced to five years in prison for his attempt to overthrow the government. While in jail, he writes *Mein Kampf* (*My Struggle*), a political manifesto that blames the Jews for rotting the social fabric of Germany. Hitler is released after eight months and starts speaking widely, strengthening the Nazi party.

1925: Meitner wins the Ignaz Lieben Prize, given by the Vienna Academy of Sciences, for her work on beta and gamma rays.

Meitner publishes sixteen articles in the past three years on atomic structure and beta and gamma rays.

Meitner and Hahn are nominated for the Nobel Prize in Chemistry.

Nazis loudly denounce "Jewish physics" as part of a "vast Semitic plot."

1926: Meitner is promoted to ausserordentlicher (exceptional) professor at the University of Berlin.

1928: Meitner, along with the French chemist Pauline Ramart-Lucas, wins the "Nobel Prize for Women," the first time the upgraded Ellen Richards Prize is given by the Association to Aid Women in Science, an American organization.

1929: Meitner and Hahn are nominated for the Nobel Prize in Chemistry.

1932: Hitler runs for the presidency of Germany and is defeated by Paul von Hindenburg, a popular military leader. Still, the Nazi party does well in the Reichstag (parliament) election.

Meitner, now a professor, at her worktable at the Berliner University, 1931

1933: Meitner and Hahn are nominated for the Nobel Prize in Chemistry.

Meitner publishes a paper with Max Delbrück on nuclear structure.

Hindenburg appoints Hitler as chancellor of a coalition government, ceding power to him.

The Reichstag fire destroys the parliament building. Hitler blames communists.

Hindenburg signs a decree, for reasons of national security, giving Hitler vast totalitarian power over the country.

The Law for the Restoration of the Professional Civil Service kicks out German Jews as "non-Aryans" (nonwhites) from all universities.

Meitner fills out a questionnaire about her race and admits to being Jewish.

Meitner's spring lecture is canceled as her fellow instructor, Leo Szilard, is Jewish and fired. Szilard leaves for England.

In late summer, Meitner's position as professor is taken away. Jews can no longer work at the university, though she continues to work in the lab at the KWI.

1934: Meitner and Hahn are nominated for the Nobel Prize in Chemistry.

Meitner convinces Hahn to start research on transuranics, following up on work started by Enrico Fermi.

President Hindenburg dies. The offices of president and chancellor are now joined into "Führer and chancellor of the Reich." Hitler takes the title and the power.

1935: Meitner and Hahn publish papers on transuranics.

The Nuremberg Laws are enacted, stripping German Jews of their citizenship and all rights.

1936: Meitner and Hahn are nominated for the Nobel Prize in Chemistry.

Meitner and Hahn publish seven more articles on their transuranic research.

1937: Meitner and Hahn are nominated for Nobel Prizes in Chemistry and Physics—the first nomination for each in physics.

1938: Germany invades Austria, unopposed. Austrians are now citizens of the Reich. Meitner, as a Jew, is now stateless, with no citizenship anywhere.

Hahn pressures Meitner to leave the KWI.

Meitner is kicked out of her apartment and moves to a hotel.

Dirk Coster, Paul Rosbaud, and Peter Debye help Meitner escape from Berlin.

Meitner settles in Stockholm.

German soldiers and civilians attack thousands of Jewish homes, businesses, and synagogues in a night of violent frenzy called Kristallnacht (Night of Broken Glass). Hundreds of Jews are killed, and 30,000 are shipped to prison camps.

Among the many new laws issued during the year and into early the next year, one demands that Jews add the name of "Sara" or "Israel" to all legal documents. Jews also are not permitted in public schools, concerts, cinemas, or parks. Jews are not allowed to own gardens. Robbing a Jew is now effectively legal, in that Jews must surrender "all jewelry of any value."

Hahn presents a puzzle he doesn't understand. Meitner realizes that the strange results of Hahn's experiments are explained by something completely unforeseen—the splitting of the atom. She and her nephew Otto Robert Frisch call this new process "nuclear fission." Hahn and Meitner write about the experiments.

1939: Meitner and Frisch publish their article on nuclear fission in *Nature*: "Disintegration of Uranium by Neutrons: A New Type of Nuclear Reaction."

Bohr opens the Fifth Washington Conference on Theoretical Physics by announcing that the atom has been split!

Germany invades Poland. Britain declares war against Germany.

1941: Meitner and Hahn are nominated for the Nobel Prizes in Physics and Chemistry.

Japan attacks Pearl Harbor, and the United States enters the war on the side of the Allies: France, Britain, and Russia.

Jews in Germany are ordered to wear the yellow star.

1942: Meitner and Hahn are nominated for the Nobel Prize in Chemistry.

1943: Meitner and Hahn are nominated for the Nobel Prize in Physics.

Meitner is invited to work on the Manhattan Project, developing and building an atomic bomb, but refuses. Many of her refugee friends work on the Manhattan Project. Only she and Albert Einstein refuse.

1944: The Allies storm the beaches of Normandy in France, a major factor in the end of the war in Europe nearly a year later. The Alsos Mission is established to follow behind the military advance, securing weapons research and scientists.

1945: The Alsos Mission captures the members of the Uranium Group, including Werner Heisenberg and Hahn.

Hitler commits suicide in an underground bunker. The Allies occupy Berlin. The war in Europe is over, with Germany divided into two parts, the eastern half controlled by the Soviets, the western half by the Americans, British, and French.

Trinity nuclear test at Jornada del Muerto desert, New Mexico, 1945

The first atomic bomb is successfully tested in the New Mexico desert near Los Alamos.

President Harry Truman orders the use of atomic bombs against Japan to force a quick end to the war.

The first atomic bomb destroys most of Hiroshima, the second Nagasaki, in Japan.

Meitner is honored as the third woman to become a foreign member of the Royal Swedish Academy of Sciences.

Meitner and Frisch are nominated for the Nobel Prize in Physics.

Hahn wins the 1944 Nobel Prize in Chemistry, awarded a year later under certain committee rules, for the discovery of nuclear fission.

1946: Meitner goes to Washington, D.C., as a visiting professor and for a speaking tour.

Meitner is given honorary doctorates at Adelphi University, the University of Rochester, Rutgers University, Smith College, and in Sweden, at Stockholm University.

Meitner and Frisch are nominated for the Nobel Prizes in Physics and Chemistry.

Meitner is named Woman of the Year at the Women's National Press Club awards ceremony.

Meitner lectures at Princeton, Harvard, MIT, Brown, and Wellesley.

1947: Meitner and Frisch are nominated for the Nobel Prizes in Chemistry and Physics.

Vienna awards Meitner the Lieber Prize for Science and Art.

Meitner accepts a salaried position in the physics department of the Royal Institute of Technology in Stockholm.

1948: Meitner and Frisch are nominated for the Nobel Prizes in Chemistry and Physics.

1949: Meitner and Hahn are honored by the German Physical Society with the Max Planck Medal. Meitner returns to Germany for the awards ceremony, the first time in ten years.

Meitner is a delegate at the United Nations' International Atomic Energy Agency.

Meitner becomes a Swedish citizen.

Lise Meitner at a blackboard, 1949

1954: Meitner retires but still lectures and works with graduate students.

The newly created Otto Hahn Prize is awarded to Meitner.

1959: Meitner attends the opening ceremony for the Hahn-Meitner Institute for Nuclear Research in West Berlin.

1960: Meitner is awarded the Wilhelm Exner Medal by the Austrian Industry Association.

Meitner moves to Cambridge, England, to be closer to Frisch and his family.

1962: The University of Göttingen awards Meitner the Dorothea Schlözer Medal.

1966: The Enrico Fermi Award is granted to Meitner, Hahn, and Strassmann by the U.S. Department of Energy.

JULY 28, 1968: Hahn dies.

OCTOBER 27, 1968: Meitner dies.

1994: Element 109 on the periodic table is named in honor of Meitner: "meitnerium."

GLOSSARY OF SELECT TERMS IN PHYSICS

ALPHA PARTICLE: A product of radioactive decay, eventually discovered to consist of two protons and two neutrons bound together to form a helium atom.

ATOMIC NUMBER: The number of protons in the nucleus of an atom, which uniquely defines what element it is.

BETA PARTICLE: A product of radioactive decay, eventually discovered to be a highly energetic electron or positron.

ELECTRON: A subatomic particle with negative electric charge, which "orbits" the nucleus instead of occupying it like protons and neutrons.

ELECTROSTATIC FORCE: Also called the Coulomb force, describes how electrically charged objects interact when still. If their charges are opposite (positive and negative), the objects experience a force attracting them to each other. If the charges are the same (positive and positive or negative and negative), the objects will be repelled from each other, much as two magnetic ends either attract or repel each other.

FISSION: The process through which a heavier, semi-stable or unstable atomic nucleus divides into two or more lighter atomic nuclei, as well as other products like subatomic particles and energy in the form of radiation.

GAMMA RAY: High-energy electromagnetic radiation caused by the radioactive decay of atomic nuclei. Unlike alpha rays, which are made up of alpha particles (helium atoms), and beta rays, which are made up of beta particles (electrons or positrons), gamma rays don't consist of particles with mass but are purely energy.

ISOTOPE: A version of an element with a different number of neutrons.

NEUTRON: A subatomic particle with no electric charge (neither positive nor negative) that occupies the nucleus of every known atom except ordinary hydrogen.

NUCLEUS: The small, dense core of an atom, consisting of at least one proton and, except for hydrogen, one neutron.

POSITRON: A particle with the same mass as an electron but the opposite charge, so it is electrically positive instead of negative.

PROTON: A subatomic particle with a positive electric charge (the opposite of an electron) that occupies the nucleus.

RADIOACTIVITY/RADIOACTIVE DECAY: The process by which unstable atomic nuclei approach stability by ejecting particles and/or radiation.

TRANSURANIC ELEMENT: Elements beyond uranium on the periodic table. This means they have more protons—are heavier—than uranium, the heaviest naturally occurring element. These elements are highly unstable and undergo radioactive decay into other, lighter elements.

PROFILES OF SCIENTISTS MENTIONED

BAGGE, ERICH (MAY 30, 1912–JUNE 5, 1996): German physicist, a student of Heisenberg, Bagge was part of the Nazis' Uranium Group working on nuclear weapons and power under Heisenberg, an unapologetic Nazi.

BOHR, NIELS (OCTOBER 7, 1885–NOVEMBER 18, 1962): Danish physicist who won the Nobel Prize in Physics in 1922 for his contributions to the understanding of atomic structure and quantum theory. Bohr was a close friend of Meitner's, helping get her out of Germany and find her a position. He worked on the Manhattan Project to develop a nuclear bomb for the Allies.

BOLTZMANN, LUDWIG (FEBRUARY 20, 1844–SEPTEMBER 5, 1906): Austrian physicist and philosopher who taught physics to Meitner at the University of Vienna.

BORN, MAX (DECEMBER 11, 1882–JANUARY 5, 1970): German Jewish physicist and mathematician who fled the Nazis, finding refuge in England. Born shared the 1954 Nobel Prize in Physics with Walther Bothe for their work on quantum mechanics.

BOSCH, CARL (AUGUST 27, 1874–APRIL 26, 1940): German chemist who won the 1931 Nobel Prize in Chemistry with Friedrich Bergius for their work on high-pressure chemistry. Bosch worked with Fritz Haber from 1909 to 1913, expanding the scale of his synthetic production of ammonia. Bosch founded IG Farben, Germany's largest chemical company. He was president of the KWI from 1937 to 1940 and tried to protect the Jewish scientists still at the institute, including Meitner.

BOTHE, WALTHER (JANUARY 8, 1891–FEBRUARY 8, 1957): German nuclear physicist who was a member of the Nazis' Uranium Group led by Heisenberg, working on nuclear weapons and power during World War II.

CHADWICK, SIR JAMES (OCTOBER 20, 1891–JULY 24, 1974): British physicist who won the 1935 Nobel Prize in Physics for his discovery of the neutron. Chadwick tried to get a place for Meitner in England but was told a Jewish woman wasn't welcome. He headed the British team that worked on the Tube Alloys Project and later joined to the Manhattan Project.

COCKCROFT, JOHN (MAY 27, 1897–SEPTEMBER 18, 1967): British physicist who won the Nobel Prize in Physics in 1951 for splitting the atomic nucleus. Cockcroft kept Meitner out of England, not trusting her as an Austrian/German refugee. During World War II, Cockcroft was assistant director of scientific research in the Ministry of Supply, focused on developing radar. He also worked on the Tube Alloys Project and was part of the MAUD Committee.

COSTER, DIRK (OCTOBER 5, 1889–FEBRUARY 12, 1950): Dutch physicist who taught at the University of Groningen for his entire career. Coster not only helped Meitner flee from Germany, but after the Nazis invaded his country, he helped other Jews hide and escape.

CURIE, MARIE (NOVEMBER 7, 1867–JULY 4, 1934): Polish physicist and chemist who immigrated to France, Curie was the first woman to win the Nobel Prize and the first person to win the Nobel Prize twice.

She won the Nobel Prize in Physics in 1903 for her work on radiation with her husband, Pierre Curie, and Henri Becquerel and the 1911 Nobel Prize in Chemistry for the discovery of radium and polonium. Meitner and Curie knew each other but weren't close, more rivals than allies.

DEBYE, PETER (MARCH 24, 1884–NOVEMBER 2, 1966): Dutch physicist and physical chemist who won the Nobel Prize in Chemistry in 1936 for his work on molecular structures. He became director of the KWI for Physics after Einstein resigned in 1934, and he helped Meitner escape from Berlin.

DELBRÜCK, MAX (SEPTEMBER 4, 1906–MARCH 9, 1981): German biophysicist who shared the 1969 Nobel Prize in Physiology or Medicine with Salvador Luria and Alfred Hershey for their research on the genetic structure of viruses. Delbrück worked as Meitner's assistant in 1932 and remained a close friend. He left Nazi Germany in 1937 for the California Institute of Technology, focusing on molecular biology, and stayed in the United States. His brother Justus and sister Emmi Bonhoeffer, as well as her husband, Klaus, and his brother, Dietrich Bonhoeffer, were involved in 1944 plots to assassinate Hitler. All except Emmi were caught and found guilty. The Bonhoeffer brothers were executed in 1945. Justus died that same year in Soviet custody.

DIEBNER, KURT (MAY 13, 1905–JULY 13, 1964): German physicist who was administrative director of the Nazis' Uranium Group, the program to work on nuclear weapons and energy under Hitler. After the war, he returned to Germany, working on using nuclear energy in ships and submarines.

EINSTEIN, ALBERT (MARCH 14, 1879–APRIL 18, 1955): German Jewish physicist who developed the theory of relativity, an important basis for quantum physics. He won the 1921 Nobel Prize in Physics. Einstein and Meitner were friends and colleagues at the KWI and almost worked together on an atomic project until they realized someone else had done the study that they were interested in. When Hitler came to power in 1933, Einstein was in the United States and chose to stay there rather than live under fascist oppression.

EKLUND, SIGVARD (JUNE 19, 1911–JANUARY 30, 2000): Swedish physicist who was director general of the International Atomic Energy Agency from 1961 to 1981. Eklund worked with Meitner to promote peaceful uses of atomic power.

FERMI, ENRICO (SEPTEMBER 29, 1901–NOVEMBER 28, 1954): Italian physicist who won the Nobel Prize in Physics in 1938 for his work on transuranics. Meitner worked on similar issues, and the two were good friends. He left Rome in 1938 when anti-Semitic laws were initiated by the Italian dictator, Benito Mussolini. His wife, Laura Capon, was Jewish. To protect her, they went to the United States, where Fermi worked on the Manhattan Project.

FISCHER, EMIL (OCTOBER 9, 1852–JULY 15, 1919): German chemist who received the 1902 Nobel Prize in Chemistry for his work on sugars and caffeine. He was at the University of Berlin from 1892 to 1919, working as director of the Chemistry Institute for the same period. Fischer's name was on the medal Hahn won while Meitner received a copy.

FOKKER, ADRIAAN (AUGUST 17, 1887–SEPTEMBER 24, 1972): Dutch physicist who studied with Einstein and Rutherford. Fokker was working in

Haarlem, the Netherlands, when he and Dirk Coster helped Meitner escape from Berlin.

FRANCK, JAMES (AUGUST 26, 1882–MAY 21, 1964): German Jewish physicist who won the 1925 Nobel Prize in Physics with Gustav Hertz, for research on the impact of electrons on atoms. Franck was a colleague of Meitner's at the KWI and a close friend throughout their lives. He resigned his position when the Nazis came to power in 1933. After a year at Niels Bohr's Institute for Theoretical Physics in Copenhagen, he left for the United States and worked on the Manhattan Project, though he strongly recommended that no bombs be used on Japanese cities without warning. His archive in Chicago contains a rich correspondence between himself and Meitner.

FRISCH, OTTO ROBERT (OCTOBER 1, 1904–SEPTEMBER 22, 1979): Austrian Jewish physicist, Meitner's nephew, who worked with her on the discovery of nuclear fission. Frisch went to England in 1939 and was there when World War II broke out. Frisch worked on the Manhattan Project, returning to England after the war to teach at Trinity College, University of Cambridge.

GEIGER, HANS (SEPTEMBER 30, 1882–SEPTEMBER 24, 1945): German physicist who co-invented the Geiger counter, used to measure radiation. Geiger was a friend of Meitner's at the KWI and part of the Nazis' Uranium Group, investigating nuclear weapons and power.

GERLACH, WALTHER (AUGUST 1, 1889–AUGUST 10, 1979): German physicist who worked in the Nazis' Uranium Group.

HABER, FRITZ (DECEMBER 9, 1868–JANUARY 29, 1934): Jewish German chemist who won the 1918 Nobel Prize in Chemistry for inventing the Haber-Bosch process, a way to synthesize ammonia from nitrogen and hydrogen gases. The process was used to manufacture both fertilizer and explosives. Haber is called the "father of chemical warfare" for his work on toxic gases used to terrifyingly lethal effect during World War I. Meitner knew and admired him at the KWI, where he was pressured to fire all Jewish employees after the Nazis came to power in 1933. Instead, he resigned as director, effective October 1933, and left the country, dying on a trip to Switzerland.

HEISENBERG, WERNER (DECEMBER 5, 1901–FEBRUARY 1, 1976): German physicist who was one of the leaders in quantum mechanics. Meitner met him early in his career and admired his work until he became an ardent Nazi. He won the Nobel Prize in Physics in 1932 for his work on quantum mechanics, particularly the uncertainty principle. In 1936, Heisenberg was attacked for his work on quantum physics as a "white Jew." Because of this taint, he lost appointments at the University of Munich. Only after Himmler, head of the SS, officially cleared Heisenberg as a "good German" could he be named director of the KWI in 1942. Heisenberg was put in charge of nuclear research under the Nazis. After being arrested by the Alsos Mission team at the end of World War II, Heisenberg was freed and settled in Göttingen, working at the newly named Max Planck Institute for Physics.

HERTZ, GUSTAV (JULY 22, 1887–OCTOBER 30, 1975): German physicist who won the 1925 Nobel Prize in Physics with James Franck. A colleague and friend of Meitner's at the KWI, he was thrown out of his position in Berlin in 1935 for being a "second-degree part-Jew," due to a Jewish grandfather (who had converted with his family to Lutheranism as a child). Hertz worked in private industry at Siemens until the anti-Jewish laws became stricter, after which he left for the Soviet Union, where he worked on the Russian nuclear project.

HERZFELD, KARL (FEBRUARY 24, 1892–JUNE 3, 1878): Austrian Jewish physicist who began his teaching career at the University of Munich. In 1926, he was offered a position at Johns Hopkins University in Baltimore, Maryland, where he taught until 1936. That year, he moved to Washington, D.C., to teach at the Catholic University of America, where he stayed until his death. Herzfeld arranged Meitner's lecture tour of the United States after the atomic bombs were detonated in Japan, ending World War II.

LAUE, MAX VON (OCTOBER 9, 1879–APRIL 24, 1960): German physicist who won the Nobel Prize in Physics in 1914 for the discovery of the diffraction of X-rays by crystals. Laue was Meitner's close colleague and friend. He strongly objected to Nazi policies but was also quick to excuse German scientists for any connection to the Third Reich. After World War II, he helped reestablish German science by clearing as many scientists as possible from the taint of Nazi association.

LAWRENCE, ERNEST (AUGUST 8, 1901–AUGUST 27, 1958): American physicist who won the Nobel Prize in Physics in 1939 for inventing the cyclotron. Lawrence cofounded the Lawrence Livermore National Laboratory with Edward Teller and worked on the Manhattan Project.

LENARD, PHILIPP (JUNE 7, 1862–MAY 20, 1947): German physicist who won the Nobel Prize in Physics in 1905 for his work on cathode rays. An early supporter of Hitler, Lenard was a vocal advocate of Nazi fascism, a loud voice condemning Jews as a cancer on German culture. Meitner was on his target list of Jewish scientists who needed to be purged. After the war, the Allies expelled him from his post as a university professor emeritus, but he was never charged for his active role in stoking hatred and violence toward Jews.

OPPENHEIMER, ROBERT (APRIL 22, 1904–FEBRUARY 18, 1967): American Jewish physicist who taught at the University of California, Berkeley, and was the wartime head of the Los Alamos Laboratory, working on the Manhattan Project.

PAULI, WOLFGANG (APRIL 25, 1900–DECEMBER 15, 1958): Austrian physicist who won the Nobel Prize in Physics in 1945 for his discovery of the exclusion principle in quantum mechanics. Pauli, Meitner's friend and colleague, wrote the famous congratulatory telegram to Coster after Meitner's escape from Berlin. He's best known for his review of Einstein's theory of relativity shortly after it came out. When Germany invaded Austria in 1938, Pauli lost his Austrian citizenship and had to leave Switzerland, where he had been a professor. With Jewish grandparents, he couldn't safely return to Hamburg. Instead, he went to the United States, working at the Institute for Advanced Study in Princeton, New Jersey, and became an American citizen.

PEIERLS, RUDOLF (JUNE 5, 1907–SEPTEMBER 19, 1995): German Jewish physicist who was at the University of Cambridge when Hitler came to power. He decided to stay in England, where he worked with Frisch at the University of Birmingham on how to use uranium in nuclear fission. Their 1940 "memorandum" was the first technical description of how to make an atomic superbomb. He also worked on the Manhattan Project, and he taught at the University of Birmingham after the war.

PLACZEK, GEORGE (SEPTEMBER 26, 1905–OCTOBER 9, 1955): Czech Jewish physicist who was a good friend of Meitner's nephew Frisch and the only one of his entire extended family to survive the Holocaust. He worked on the Manhattan Project and, after the war, had a position at the Institute for Advanced Study in Princeton, New Jersey.

PLANCK, MAX (APRIL 23, 1858–OCTOBER 4, 1947): German physicist who discovered energy quanta–that energy is emitted in discrete units. Planck won the 1918 Nobel Prize in Physics for this research. Meitner moved to Berlin to work with Planck. He taught at the University of Berlin from 1889 to 1926 and hired Meitner as a teaching assistant. In 1948, the Kaiser Wilhelm Society was renamed the Max Planck Society.

RAMART-LUCAS, PAULINE (NOVEMBER 22, 1880–MARCH 17, 1953): French chemist who taught at the University of Paris from 1935 to 1941 and again from 1944 until her death in 1953; she was the second woman scientist at the Sorbonne after Marie Curie. During the war, she was a vocal anti-fascist and was kicked out of her position by the Vichy government (the appeasing French government during the German occupation). Along with Meitner, she was awarded the upgraded Ellen Richards Prize, the "Nobel Prize for Women."

RUBENS, HEINRICH (MARCH 30, 1865–JULY 17, 1922): German physicist who taught at the University of Berlin from 1906 on. He was named director of the KWI in 1906. Rubens oversaw Meitner's work when she first arrived in Berlin, insisting she work with no title and no pay in the basement, apart from the men.

RUTHERFORD, ERNEST (AUGUST 30, 1871–OCTOBER 19, 1937): Physicist from New Zealand who did his major research first in Canada, then in

England. Known as the "father of nuclear physics," he won the 1908 Nobel Prize in Chemistry for his work on radioactive disintegration or "half-life." Hahn was a student under Rutherford and introduced Meitner to his professor, who had assumed she must be a man, given the work she had done.

SCHERRER, PAUL (FEBRUARY 3, 1890–SEPTEMBER 25, 1969): Swiss physicist who taught at ETH Zurich for forty years. Scherrer helped organize Meitner's escape from Berlin.

SIEGBHAN, MANNE (DECEMBER 3, 1886–SEPTEMBER 26, 1978): Swedish physicist who won the Nobel Prize in Physics in 1924 for his work on X-ray spectroscopy. In 1937, he was named director of what was generally referred to in English as the Nobel Institute of Physics, established by the Royal Swedish Academy of Sciences. Siegbahn gave Meitner a position as a refugee but not much support.

STARK, JOHANNES (APRIL 15, 1874–JUNE 21, 1957): German physicist who won the Nobel Prize in Physics in 1919 for discovering the Doppler effect in canal rays. Along with Philipp Lenard, Stark was a rabid anti-Semite who argued loudly for the removal of Jews from every aspect of German life, especially the sciences. Meitner was on his list of "undesirables." In 1947, he was found guilty of being a "Major Offender" by a court ordered to purge Nazis from postwar German academia. He was sentenced to four years in prison, but the sentence was suspended, and he lived out the rest of his life in peaceful retirement.

STERN, OTTO (FEBRUARY 17, 1888–AUGUST 17, 1969): German Jewish physicist who worked with Meitner's nephew Frisch. In 1933, after the Nazi takeover of the government, Stern resigned his post and left Germany for the United States. He became a professor of physics at the Carnegie Institute of Technology and won the Nobel Prize in Physics in 1943 for his work on the molecular ray method.

STRASSMANN, FRITZ (FEBRUARY 22, 1902–APRIL 22, 1980): German chemist who worked at the KWI from 1929 to 1946. Strassmann worked with Hahn and Meitner from 1933 until their shared discovery of nuclear fission in 1939. In 1985, Strassmann and his wife, Maria, were recognized as "Righteous Among the Nations" by Yad Vashem, the World Holocaust Remembrance Center in Jerusalem, for risking their lives by hiding a Jewish woman in their home.

SZILARD, LEO (FEBRUARY 11, 1898–MAY 30, 1964): Hungarian Jewish physicist who taught classes with Meitner in Berlin. When Hitler became chancellor, Szilard left for England, and later he moved to the United States. In 1939, he wrote the famous letter Albert Einstein signed to convince President Roosevelt to start the Manhattan Project, which Szilard then worked on.

TELLER, EDWARD (JANUARY 15, 1908–SEPTEMBER 9, 2003): Jewish Hungarian physicist who cofounded the Lawrence Livermore National Laboratory in California with Ernest Lawrence and was its director, then assistant director, for nearly twenty years. Teller left Hungary in 1926 due to anti-Semitism, going to Germany to complete his studies. When Hitler took power in 1933, Teller left for Copenhagen, working with Niels Bohr, then went to England in 1934. In 1942, he joined work on the Manhattan Project. Teller was one of the first scientists to warn about the catastrophic effects of global warming caused by burning fossil fuels, sounding the alarm in 1957.

THOMSON, J. J. (DECEMBER 18, 1856–AUGUST 30, 1940): British physicist who won the Nobel Prize in Physics in 1906 for discovering the electron, the first subatomic particle to be found. Thomson taught physics at the University of Cambridge from 1884 until his death. Besides being a brilliant researcher, he was an inspiring teacher, paving the way for more Nobel laureates, including Rutherford, Bohr, and Born. Thomson posited the model of the atom as a plum pudding, a version corrected by Rutherford and then Bohr. Thomson was knighted in 1908 and buried in Westminster Abbey, near the grave of Sir Isaac Newton.

UBISCH, GERTA VON (OCTOBER 3, 1882–MARCH 31, 1965): Jewish German physicist, geneticist, and botanist. Ubisch studied at the University of Berlin, where she made Meitner feel more welcome. The two wrote to each other throughout their lives. Ubisch moved to Heidelberg University to continue her doctorate. She started teaching at Heidelberg in 1923, the first woman to do so at that university, among the first in all of Germany. In 1933, she lost her faculty position because she was Jewish. In 1934, she left Germany for the Netherlands and Switzerland. The following year, she moved to Brazil, where she worked in São Paulo. She returned to Germany in 1952, applying for financial compensation for her losses under the Nazis. She fought for reparations for ten years but was denied, dying penniless.

WEIZSÄCKER, CARL FRIEDRICH VON (JUNE 28, 1912–APRIL 28, 2007): German physicist who worked in the Nazis' Uranium Group with Heisenberg during World War II. Weizsäcker went with Heisenberg on the famous trip to Copenhagen to question Bohr about nuclear weapons research. His recorded conversations while detained at Farm Hall in England for months after the war reveal a strong defense of Germany as morally superior to Americans and an unwillingness to admit any of the crimes perpetuated by the Nazis. After the war, Weizsäcker was made director of the physics department at the Max Planck Institute. From 1970 to 1980, he was the founding director of the Max Planck Institute for the Study of Living Conditions in the Scientific and Technical World (later renamed the Max Planck Institute for Social Sciences), in Starnberg.

WIGNER, EUGENE (NOVEMBER 17, 1902–JANUARY 1, 1995): Jewish Hungarian physicist who won the Nobel Prize in Physics in 1963 for work on the theory of the atomic nucleus. He worked with Szilard to convince Einstein to sign the letter urging President Roosevelt to develop a nuclear weapon and led his own team on the Manhattan Project.

WIRTZ, KARL (APRIL 24, 1910–FEBRUARY 12, 1994): German physicist who was Meitner's colleague and later part of the Nazis' Uranium Group working on nuclear weapons and power. After being released from internment at Farm Hall in England, he returned to work at the Max Planck Institute (previously the KWI), then taught at the Universities of Göttingen and Karlsruhe.

NOTES

ONE: DREAMS OF THE IMPOSSIBLE

2 "excited that there were such things to find out about in our world": Meitner, "Lise Meitner Looks Back," *Bulletin of the Atomic Scientists* 20, no. 9 (November 1964): 2.

2 "the character of the university would be lost and the institution endangered": Ruth Lewin Sime, *Lise Meitner: A Life in Physics* (Berkeley: University of California Press, 1996), p. 25.

2 "Listen to your father and me, but think for yourself": Ibid., p. 9.

3 "you've just walked across the room without picking up a book": Ibid., p. 9.

TWO: EDUCATION AT LAST!

6 "the most beautiful and stimulating that I have ever heard . . . a completely new and wonderful world had been revealed": Sime, *Lise Meitner,* p. 13.

6 "Boltzmann gave her the vision of physics as a battle for ultimate truth": Otto Robert Frisch, quoted in ibid., p. 17.

THREE: A PROFESSOR WITH NO PROFESSION

8 "I admire your courage": Charles Chiu, *Women in the Shadows* (New York: Peter Lang, 2008), p. 89.

9 “would not think of printing an article written by a woman!”: Sime, *Lise Meitner*, p. 36.

10 “bordering on fear of people”: Ibid., p. 24.

10 “Women’s education was just beginning to develop . . . able to become a scientist”: Meitner, “Lise Meitner Looks Back,” p. 6.

10 “He received me very kindly . . . at the time”: Sime, *Lise Meitner*, p. 24.

11 “keeping women from universities is an injustice that has gone on far too long”: Ibid., p. 25.

FOUR: A PARTNERSHIP BETTER THAN MARRIAGE

15 “This group of young physicists . . . a friendly manner into this circle”: Meitner, “Lise Meitner Looks Back,” p. 9.

FIVE: THE NEW SCIENCE OF RADIOACTIVITY

17 “There was no question . . . yet we were really very close friends”: Otto Hahn, *My Life: The Autobiography of a Scientist* (London: Macdonald, 1970), p. 88.

20 “I love physics . . . grateful for many things”: Sime, *Lise Meitner*, p. 45.

SIX: OUT OF THE DARK

21 “Oh, I thought you were a man!”: Meitner, “Lise Meitner Looks Back,” p. 5.

21 "Sometimes I lack courage . . . almost unbearable to me": Meitner to Steinman, Associated Papers of Lise Meitner, Churchill Archives Centre, Churchill College, University of Cambridge (hereafter Meitner Papers).

23 "One should think of matter as condensed energy": Deborah Crawford, *Lise Meitner, Atomic Pioneer* (New York: Crown, 1969), p. 57.

23 "Since the velocity of light . . . $E=mc^2$": Ibid., p. 58.

23 "I almost understood him!": Ibid., p. 58.

23 "At that time . . . I remember the lecture well.:" Meitner, "Lise Meitner Looks Back," p. 4.

24 "Not only did this give me a chance . . . prejudices against academic women": Meitner, "The Status of Women in the Professions," *Physics Today* 13, no. 8 (August 1960): 20.

SEVEN: WAR AND SCIENCE

27 "You can hardly imagine my way of life . . . nor will again": Meitner to Hahn, literary estate of Otto Hahn, Archives of the Max Planck Society, Berlin-Dahlem.

28 "Warfare cannot be humanized. It can only be abolished": Bretislav Friedrich, "A Brief Biography of Fritz Haber (1868–1934)," Fritz Haber Institute, February 20, 2016, p. 17 www.fhi.mpg.de/70309/History_Brief_Bio_Haber.pdf.

29 "Some got away . . . to die better": Patricia Rife, *Lise Meitner and the Dawn of the Nuclear Age* (Boston: Birkhäuser, 1999), p. 70.

30 "You have told us . . . on enemy soldiers": Ibid., p. 70.

31 "ashamed . . . very much upset": Hahn, *My Life*, p. 122.

31 "As a result . . . receiving end": Ibid., pp. 122–23.

NINE: AFTER THE WAR

37 "There really is enough to eat . . . hardly any butter": Sime, *Lise Meitner*, p. 98.

TEN: A PROFESSOR AT LAST

42 "life need not be easy . . . this wish I have been granted": Meitner, "Lise Meitner Looks Back," p. 2.

43 "When James Franck . . . we had understood very little": Ibid., p. 11.

ELEVEN: "JEWISH" PHYSICS VS. "ARYAN" PHYSICS

45 "We need lucid minds . . . root of scientific perversion, of evil!": Philipp Lenard, "A Big Day for Science: Johannes Stark Appointed President of the Reich Physical and Technical Institute," *Völkischer Beobachter*, May 13, 1933, reprinted in *Physics and National Socialism: An Anthology of Primary Sources*, ed. Klaus Hentschel, trans. Ann M. Hentschel (1996; repr., Basel: Springer, 2011), p. 50.

47 "The scientific irrefutability . . . devotion to truth": Rife, *Lise Meitner*, p. 135.

47 "Bring forward . . . defend it to your last breath!": S. Rajasekar and N. Athavan, "Ludwig Edward Boltzmann," Cornell University, 2006, p. 14, arXiv: physics/0609047.

TWELVE: HITLER TAKES POWER

50 "These sub-humans . . . hear nothing of the cheering from the masses": Robert Gellately, *Backing Hitler: Consent and Coercion in Nazi Germany* (Oxford: Oxford University Press, 2001), p. 18.

50 "The only who really knows . . . he slapped his thigh": Transcript, Nuremberg Trials, March 18, 1946, in Trial of the Major War Criminals Before the International Military Tribunal, vol. 9 (Nuremberg: IMT, 1947).

52 "As long as the possibility . . . the cause of international understanding are being persecuted": Armin Hermann, *The New Physics: The Route into the Atomic Age* (Bonn: Inter Nationes, 1979), p. 75.

52 "atrocity campaign against Germany": Ibid., p. 75.

THIRTEEN: BOYCOTT THE JEWS!

53 "Jews have destroyed German businesses . . . Jews are our disaster!": anti-Semitic signs, United States Holocaust Memorial Museum, Washington, D.C.

53 "sensationalize German persecution of the Jews": Rife, *Lise Meitner*, p. 113.

55 "a competent scientist . . . blocking the path to advancement for many promising German ['Aryan'] scientists": Ibid., pp. 136–37.

56 "It was . . . my life's work, and it seemed terribly hard to separate myself from it": Meitner to Gerta von Ubisch, July 1, 1947, Meitner Papers.

FOURTEEN: A TALK WITH HITLER ABOUT SCIENCE

57 "But what can I do? . . . can something so lawless be a law?": Sime, *Lise Meitner*, p. 142.

57 "There are no good Jews! . . . you find others": Max Planck, "My Audience with Adolf Hitler, [May 6, 1947]," in *Hentschel, Physics and National Socialism*, p. 359.

57 "No! . . . There is no Jewish worthiness": Ibid.

57 "People say I suffer . . . I have nerves of steel!": Ibid.

58 "lived almost like a saint": Sime, *Lise Meitner*, p. 144.

58 "Take a pleasant trip abroad . . . will have disappeared": Sime, *Lise Meitner*, p. 148.

59 "They all thought . . . the moral point of view was completely absent or very weak": Spencer R. Weart and Gertrud Weiss Szilard, eds., *Leo Szilard: His Version of the Facts; Selected Recollections and Correspondence* (Cambridge, Mass.: MIT Press, 1980), pp. 13–14.

FIFTEEN: TO GO OR TO STAY

61 "With the massive introduction of Jews . . . Mr. Einstein with his 'theories.'": Lenard, "A Big Day for Science," p. 50.

SIXTEEN: THE NAZIFICATION OF SCIENCE

65 "unpleasant, thankless task": Hahn, *My Life*, p. 50.

65 "The presence of . . . my length of service": Ibid., p. 53.

65 "painful experiences": Ibid., p. 146.

66 "the Jewess endangers the Institute:" Sime, *Lise Meitner*, p. 184.

67 "She was the true life and soul of the Institute": Rife, *Lise Meitner*, p. 136.

69 "I will perform the ceremony, unless I am taken away by the police": Hermann, *The New Physics*, p. 86.

69 "excited and pleased . . . prevent us from entering by force": Ibid., p. 86.

70 "All members of [KWI] . . . for the Jew Fritz Haber": Ibid., p. 86.

70 "The lovely large reception hall . . . of World War I": Friedrich, "A Brief Biography of Fritz Haber," pp. 1–2.

SEVENTEEN: CAN IT GET WORSE?

73 "H[eisenberg] was by then a professor . . . And my poor Max wept": Arnold Kramish, *The Griffin: The Greatest Untold Espionage Story of World War II* (Boston: Houghton Mifflin, 1986), p. 44.

EIGHTEEN: THE NEW RADIOACTIVE PHYSICS

77 "one hears only my name . . . which is not mine exclusively": Hahn to Rudolf Pummerer, October 13, 1936, in Rife, *Lise Meitner*, p. 148.

NINETEEN: THE JEWESS MUST GO

79 "In July of last year . . . spheres of national life": Rife, *Lise Meitner*, pp. 161–62.

80 "Hahn says I should not come to the Institute anymore": Kitty Ferguson, *Lost Science: Astonishing Tales of Forgotten Genius* (New York: Sterling, 2017), p. 194.

80 "He has in essence thrown me out": Ibid., p. 194.

80 "Lise was very unhappy . . . had left her in the lurch": Hahn, *My Life*, p. 53.

81 "In almost no other science . . . Niels David Bohr": Ludwig Glaser, "Jews in Physics: Jewish Physics, [November 1939]," in Hentschel, *Physics & National Socialism*, pp. 223, 226–27.

82 "Miss Meitner is non-Aryan . . . Heil Hitler!": Rife, *Lise Meitner*, p. 165.

83 "By order of the Reichminister . . . of the German sciences": Ibid., p. 166.

TWENTY: PASSPORT PROBLEMS

85 "Went for information . . . will not be permitted to get out": Rife, *Lise Meitner*, p. 167.

89 "in order": Ibid., p. 170.

90 "The assistant we talked about . . . my wife and me even greater pleasure": Ibid., p. 171.

91 "Sat 9 July . . . back with me": Ibid., p. 171.

TWENTY-ONE: HOW TO SMUGGLE A SCIENTIST

92 "Without answer from Coster/clarification urgently requested": Rife, *Lise Meitner*, p. 171.

92 "Coster on his way": Ibid., p. 172.

96 "urgent emergencies": Ibid., p. 172.

TWENTY-TWO: SUCCESS OR FAILURE?

99 "With fear and trembling we wondered . . . arrested on trains and brought back": Hahn, *My Life*, p. 149.

TWENTY-THREE: A NARROW ESCAPE

102 "inwardly torn apart": Rife, *Lise Meitner*, p. 173.

102 "You have made yourself as famous for the abduction of Lise Meitner as for [the discovery of] hafnium!": Ibid., p. 174.

103 "The shot that was to bring you down . . . you had arrived safely": Ibid., p. 173.

106 "Professor Lise Meitner . . . percentage of Jewish blood she has": Ibid., p. 175.

106 "Perhaps you cannot fully appreciate . . . I am very lonely": Meitner to Hahn, September 25, 1938, Ibid., p. 179.

107 "I feel like a wind-up doll . . . has no real life in itself": Hermann, *The New Physics*, p. 93.

107 "One dare not look back. One cannot look forward": Sime, *Lise Meitner*, p. 209.

109 "Scientifically I am completely isolated . . . you cannot call it work": Ibid., p. 280.

TWENTY-FOUR: A BRILLIANT ENOUGH PHYSICIST?

113 "My very own life . . . waits longingly for news": Meitner to Elizabeth Schiemann, November 29, 1938–October 1939, Meitner Papers.

TWENTY-FIVE: AN ATOMIC MYSTERY

115 "What shall I write? . . . It means almost nothing to me anymore": Meitner to Elizabeth Schiemann, November 29, 1938–October 1939, Meitner Papers.

115 "The thing is . . . we must clear this up": Rife, *Lise Meitner*, p. 185.

117 "We've had so many surprises . . . can't very well say it is impossible": Ibid., pp. 185–86.

117 "From these experiments . . . an unusual series of accidents": Ibid., p. 187.

TWENTY-SIX: THE ATOM SPLITS!

119 "There is not the slightest indication that the energy . . . the atom itself would have to shatter or dissolve": Crawford, *Lise Meitner*, p. 35.

121 "The charge of a uranium nucleus . . . impact of a single neutron": Otto Robert Frisch, *What Little I Remember* (Cambridge: Cambridge University Press, 1980), p. 116.

122 "we had been blinded by 'the rules' . . . no other solution would fit": Ibid., p. 140.

TWENTY-SEVEN: THE IMPOSSIBLE IS POSSIBLE!

123 "I believed it was only theoretically possible . . . Meitner who provided the correct interpretation": Albert Einstein, *Out of My Later Years* (New York: Gramercy, 1993), p. 188.

123 "What fools we've been! We ought to have seen that before!": Lawrence Badash, Elizabeth Hodes, and Adolph Tiddens, "Nuclear Fission: Reaction to the Discovery in 1939," *Proceedings of the American Philosophical Society* 130, no. 2 (June 1986): p. 208.

123 "Every great and deep difficulty . . . in order to find it": Michael F. L'Annunziata, *Radioactivity: Introduction and History*. p. 397

125 "I have totally retracted . . . really is a wonderful thing": Rife, *Lise Meitner*, p. 203.

127 "It seems therefore possible . . . equal size": *Nature* 143, no. 3615 (February 11, 1939): p. 202.

127 "Anyone who says that . . . is talking moonshine": Ibid., p. 211.

127 "The more our knowledge of nuclear reactions advances . . . seems to become": Niels Bohr, "Neutron Capture and Nuclear Constitution," *Nature* 137, no. 3461 (February 29, 1936): 348.

128 "Last week the Hahn report . . . announced confirmation": "Science: Great Accident," *Time*, February 6, 1939, p. 21.

128 "I don't feel at all happy . . . I am losing all my courage": Meitner to Hahn, March 1939, in Rife, *Lise Meitner*, pp. 211–12.

130 "owed nothing to physics!": Ibid., p. 213.

TWENTY-EIGHT: THE POWER OF NUCLEAR FISSION

131 "Nuts!": Weart and Szilard, *Leo Szilard*, p. 37.

133 "My work is equivalent to zero": Meitner to Hahn, October 27, 1939, in Rife, *Lise Meitner*, p. 220.

134 "Why should Hitler occupy Denmark? He can just telephone, can't he?": Frisch, *What Little I Remember*, p. 108.

136 "he is ready at any time to defend Germany . . . Jewish influence into the German living space": "SS Head of the Central Office of Public Safety: Letter to Rudolf Mentzel Enclosing Report on Heisenberg, [May 26, 1939]," in Hentschel, *Physics and National Socialism*, p. 197.

TWENTY-NINE: A LETTER FROM EINSTEIN

138 "I never thought of that!" Weart and Szilard, *Leo Szilard*, p. 38.

138 "The one thing that most scientists . . . position unique on this occasion": Ibid., p. 339.

139 "speed up the experimental work . . . have the necessary equipment": Ibid, p. 40.

141 "In two weeks . . . right now it makes me feel pretty low": Sime, *Lise Meitner*, p. 270.

THIRTY: THE RACE FOR THE BOMB

142 "We were all much relieved . . . he doesn't have it in view to give up his work": Kramish, *The Griffin*, p. 86.

145 "not completely free . . . also not completely free": Rife, *Lise Meitner*, p. 228.

THIRTY-ONE: A LAB OF ONE'S OWN

147 "Hitler had sometimes spoken to me . . . bombs against England": Rife, *Lise Meitner*, p. 233.

149 "Half amusing and half depressing . . . They have gone astray": Kramish, *The Griffin*, pp. 120–21.

149 "unforgivable": Ibid., p. 121.

150 "I am afraid that the Allies have no such man as Heisenberg": Ibid., p. 194.

150 "I will have nothing to do with a bomb!": Sime, *Lise Meitner*, p. 305.

152 "It is significant that Hitler . . . his lack of understanding of fundamental scientific research": Rife, *Lise Meitner*, p. 239.

THIRTY-TWO: ANOTHER PHYSICIST ESCAPES

155 "He came at the right moment . . . that were left unanswered before": Leslie Groves. *Now It Can Be Told: The Story of the Manhattan Project* (New York: Da Capo, 1983), p. 198.

THIRTY-THREE: THE GERMAN NUCLEAR PROGRAM

158 "it was possible to surmount the technical difficulties involved": Rife, *Lise Meitner,* p. 245.

159 "This courageous deed . . . would not have dared to do it": Kramish, *The Griffin,* p. 221.

THIRTY-FOUR: WHAT TO DO WITH NAZI SCIENTISTS?

162 "I wonder whether . . . old fashioned in that respect": *Operation Epsilon: The Farm Hall Transcripts* (Berkeley: University of California Press, 1993), p. 33.

165 "Dear Otto . . . here is an attempt to help you all. With very affectionate greetings to everyone. Yours, Meitner": Meitner to Hahn, June 27, 1945, in Hentschel, *Physics and National Socialism,* pp. 332–34.

167 "in 1938 when the non-Aryan . . . keep her in my Institute": *Operation Epsilon,* p. 75.

168 "He says every day . . . as he has here": *Operation Epsilon,* p. 49.

168 "If Hitler ordered a few atrocities . . . they can't do the same things to us now": *Operation Epsilon,* p. 50.

168 "We have done things . . . what we did": *Operation Epsilon*, p. 55.

169 "We must tell the Americans . . . to make the bomb": *Operation Epsilon*, p. 50.

169 "A letter that did not reach him": Kramish, *The Griffin*, p. 127.

THIRTY-FIVE: THE MOTHER OF THE BOMB

171 "brilliant mathematician": Lise Meitner, interview, *Saturday Evening Post*, 1946, in Crawford, *Lise Meitner*, p. 176.

171 "I must stress . . . put our discoveries": Ibid., p. 175.

172 "When I read the dramatic . . . war to a close": Ibid., p. 161.

173 "I agree . . . peaceful work": Ibid., p. 161.

173 "peaceful work": Rife, *Lise Meitner*, p. 253.

173 "It could be used to drive submarines, aircraft, and industrial power": Crawford, *Lise Meitner*, p. 164.

173 "What I do know now! . . . has become inconceivable reality": Meitner to Elizabeth Schiemann, Meitner Papers.

THIRTY-SIX: THE AMERICANS DID WHAT?!

174 "All I can suggest . . . doesn't work at all": *Operation Epsilon*, p. 71.

174 "I'm willing to believe . . . to do with uranium": Ibid., p. 72.

174 "I think it's dreadful of the Americans . . . madness on their part": Ibid., p. 72.

174 "One can't say that . . . quickest way of ending the war": Ibid., p. 72.

174 "Well, how have they actually done it . . . work out how they did it": Ibid., p. 118.

174 "The point is . . . get it through": Ibid., p. 77.

175 "History will record . . . this ghastly weapon of war": Ibid., p. 92.

176 He has been very shattered . . . at the time of the discovery": Ibid., p. 97.

177 "The Hahn discovery . . . herself in the discover": Ibid., p.105.

177 "I still do not understand what they have done": Ibid., p. 117.

THIRTY-SEVEN: MEITNER IN AMERICA

179 "Ah, so you're the little lady who got us into this mess!": Meitner, "*Lise Meitner Looks Back*"," p. 4.

180 "Groves told me that . . . theoretical physicists are prima donnas": Sime, *Lise Meitner*, p. 333.

180 "I felt that the manner . . . off any questions from me": Ibid., p. 333.

THIRTY-EIGHT: THE NOBEL PRIZE FOR NUCLEAR FISSION GOES TO . . .

182 "Hahn came to see me . . . left the room abruptly": *Operation Epsilon*, p. 262.

183 "It would be a mistake . . . everything has been": Ibid., p. 274.

183 "Yes, that should be avoided . . . extremely well": Ibid., p. 274.

185 "forgetting the past . . . his life's work": Meitner to James Franck, January 16, 1946, in Charlotte Kerner, *Lise, Atomphysikerin: Die Lebensgeschichte der Lise Meitner* (Weinheim, Germany: Beltz und Gelberg, 1998), p. 111 n. 1.

185 "I had quite an unhappy conversation . . . with my colleague Fritz Strassmann": Sime, *Lise Meitner*, p. 342.

THIRTY-NINE: AFTER THE WAR: WORKING FOR NUCLEAR PEACE

187 "He suppresses the Nazi crimes:" letter to sister Lola, Sime, *Lise Meitner*, pp. 345.

187 "I find it quite painful . . . work together": Meitner to Bahr-Bergius, December 24, 1946, in ibid., p. 344.

189 "the Germans have still not understood . . . I would not be able to breathe in this atmosphere": Chiu, *Women in the Shadows*, p. 105.

189 "It is clear to me that Hahn . . . an especially gruesome expression in nazism": Meitner to James Franck, January 16, 1947, in Sime, *Lise Meitner*, p. 345.

189 "One cannot do anything . . . also for the German people": Hahn to Meitner, June 16, 1948, in ibid., p. 356.

190 "Is it really justifiable . . . but risks achieving the opposite": Meitner to Hahn, June 6, 1948, in Hentschel, *Physics and National Socialism*, p. 402.

191 "in part because . . . no objections to Austrians": Meitner to Franck, summer 1948, in Sime, *Lise Meitner*, p. 357.

191 "Those who remained . . . 'She didn't really EARN her place here'": Meitner to Hahn, Meitner Papers.

FORTY: A PRIZE OF HER OWN

193 "What would you say . . . past also be taken from me?": Rife, *Lise Meitner*, pp. 264–65.

194 "Now, dear Lise . . . buy me a beer!": Werner Stolz, *Otto Hahn/Lise Meitner*, (Wiesbaden: Vieweg + Teubner Verlag, 1989), p. 78 (my translation).

SELECT BIBLIOGRAPHY

Cassidy, David C. *Farm Hall and the German Atomic Project of World War II: A Dramatic History*. Cham, Switzerland: Springer, 2017.

Chiu, Charles. *Women in the Shadows*. New York: Peter Lang, 2008.

Crawford, Deborah. *Lise Meitner, Atomic Pioneer*. New York: Crown, 1969.

Frank, Sir Charles. *Operation Epsilon: The Farm Hall Transcripts*. Berkeley: University of California Press, 1993.

Kramish, Arnold. *The Griffin: The Greatest Untold Espionage Story of World War II*. Boston: Houghton Mifflin, 1986.

Meitner, Lise. "Lise Meitner Looks Back." *Bulletin of the Atomic Scientists* 20, no. 9 (November 1964): 2–7.

——. "The Status of Women in the Professions." *Physics Today* 13, no. 8 (August 1960): 16–21.

Rife, Patricia. *Lise Meitner and the Dawn of the Nuclear Age*. Boston: Birkhäuser, 1999.

Sime, Ruth Lewin. *Lise Meitner: A Life in Physics*. Berkeley: University of California Press, 1996.

IMAGE CREDITS

Page 196: "Nuclear Fission Deutsches Museum" via brewbooks/Flickr, licensed under CC BY-SA 2.0. **Pages 198–99:** From the Archives of the Max Planck Society, Berlin. **Page 200:** The Papers of Lise Meitner, MTNR 8/5/1; photograph of Lise Meitner in winter garden, Vienna, 1899, Churchill Archives Centre. **Page 202:** From the Archives of the Max Planck Society, Berlin. **Page 203:** From the Archives of the Max Planck Society, Berlin. **Page 204:** Heka Davis, Nuclear Regulatory Commission Archive, Library of Congress. **Page 209:** From the Archives of the Max Planck Society, Berlin. **Page 213:** Digital Photo Archive, Department of Energy (DOE), courtesy of AIP Emilio Segrè Visual Archives. **Page 215:** The Papers of Lise Meitner, MTNR 8/4/14; photograph of Lise Meitner at a blackboard, 1949, Churchill Archives Centre.

ACKNOWLEDGMENTS

Thanks first to Warren Heckrotte, nuclear physicist and friend, who guided me through the thornier thickets of nuclear science. I'm also grateful to Asa Stahl, a PhD student in physics at Rice University, who generously read the completed manuscript and helped clarify the scientific descriptions and concepts.

Like many writers, I rely on a group of fellow writers to read and criticize my pages. I owe them all for their insightful comments: Gennifer Choldenko, Diane Fraser, Elizabeth Partridge, Emily Polsby, and Pamela Turner. Joan Lester, another fellow writer, also critiqued many versions. It truly takes a village to get a book out into the world, and I'm fortunate to have such a supportive one.

INDEX

Note: Page numbers in *italics* refer to illustrations.